CHURCH GROWTH UNLEASHED

For foreign and subsidiary rights, contact the author.

Cover design by Sara Young

ISBN: 978-1-962401-46-3   1 2 3 4 5 6 7 8 9 10

Printed in the United States of America

WHAT PEOPLE ARE SAYING ABOUT
CHURCH GROWTH UNLEASHED

A book on growing a church from someone who's actually done it. Danny provides the why, how, and what on growing your church in today's culture. Reignite your ambition, passion, and vision for reaching more people with the hope of Jesus and making a bigger impact!

—Brad Lomenick
Founder, BLINC
Author, H3 Leadership & The Catalyst Leader
BradLomenick.com

Amidst the abundance of church growth books, *Church Growth Unleashed* stands out as a beacon of hope and wisdom. In a world where too many families bear the weight of sacrifices made for the sake of ministry, Danny Anderson's message resonates deeply.

His insightful approach to church growth not only offers strategies for expanding congregations but crucially emphasizes nurturing one's relationship with God and preserving family bonds along the way. In an era where pastors often trade what is truly valuable for worldly acclaim, Danny's reminder that church growth can coexist with spiritual fulfillment and family harmony is a timely and essential message.

Church Growth Unleashed is not just a roadmap for expanding churches; it's a guide to cultivating healthier souls and families in the process.

—Brent McQuay
Lead Pastor Christian Life Center Tinley Park IL, CLC.tv

Danny does a great job reminding us all: The main thing is still the main thing. . . . it's impossible to lead people to a place you've never been. Ministry isn't just about tasks, strategies, and stuff. It's about a work of God inside us that overflows in how we lead, and that begins with my own soul and my family. Our leadership (and the results) won't grow (and sustain) beyond that ceiling. I love Danny's transparency and authenticity, and his direct challenge is a must-read for leaders in today's church.

—Jason King
Lead Pastor, Bayside Baptist Church, BaysideBaptist.org

Danny's message matches his life. His longstanding pursuit of Jesus and the lost in a life-giving way have afforded ministry depth and breadth. In *Church Growth Unleashed*, he lays a timely pathway with fresh application of timeless truths. It will affirm, renew, and equip you as you pursue God's work God's way. If you're looking for accessible practices that will help you hold onto your soul while extending the arms of Jesus, this book is for you.

I respect and value Danny. He's a godly leader, Christ-like example, faithful ministry partner, and friend. My endorsement is both personal and professional as much can be gained from the book and the life behind it.

—Micah McElveen
Vapor Ministries, VaporMinistries.org

Pastor Danny Anderson's *Church Growth Unleashed* is a must-read for pastors aspiring to finish their journey with greater strength than they began. Danny illustrates from his own journey that tending to a healthy soul, nurturing a thriving marriage, and cherishing family relationships are not incompatible with leading a growing church. Through practical strategies and profound insights, this book serves as a beacon, guiding pastors toward being all that God has created them to be so they can do all that God has created them to do. Within these pages lies the hope of a flourishing soul and a thriving church.

—Daniel Butson
Lead Pastor, Fellowship Church, FishHawkFC.org

When I read this book, I was immediately struck by the significance of the message. As the lead pastor of a growing church, I have personally felt the tension that Danny Anderson brings to light concerning church leaders maintaining their health as they lead thriving, growing communities of faith.

As Pastor Danny points out, God intends for our churches to grow, and our world has never needed healthy pastors to lead those growing churches more than we do right now. In this enlightening, easy-to-read book, Danny helps guide us toward sustained church growth while remaining saved and sane. He shows us that we do not have to sacrifice our marriages, our relationships with our children, or our health to build the Kingdom of God.

—Jonathan Moore
Lead Pastor, Northrock Church, NorthRockSA.com

Church Growth Unleashed is personal, practical, and written straight to the heart of every pastor. As a pastor myself, I identify with Danny's encouragement to regularly assess the condition of and to nurture my own soul first, in order to lead my church well.

Danny's own experience informs this compelling narrative and passes to us the inspiring truth that it is possible to grow our churches without losing our souls!

—Zach Swift
Lead Pastor, West Hill Baptist Church, MyWestHill.church

Danny is a fresh voice every pastor needs to hear in the pages of this book. I can personally vouch for the fact that Danny actually has the moral authority to write the words contained herein. I have watched as he lived out these pages. Read and listen closely. This could grow your ministry, but could also potentially save your ministry. . . . and your life!

—Shawn Lovejoy
Founder & CEO, CourageToLead

Danny Anderson is a present-day voice with an 'early church' heart and mind. He is a pastor's pastor; one who has been through the refining fire and is willing to lead you through it. His message of "soul care" and "family ministry" to the leadership of the church today is right on time. Danny's challenge for us, as ministers, to care for our souls and homes is of utmost importance for our own survival and well-being.

–Jeff Williams
Lead Pastor, Southside Church in
Athens, GA / Southside.online

CHURCH GROWTH UNLEASHED

How to Grow Your Church Without Losing Your Soul

Danny Anderson

ARROWS & STONES

This book is dedicated to all the pastors who desire to grow their church by reaching their communities with the Good News of the Gospel. May the words and insights in these pages offer you guidance and wisdom on your journey, so that you may finish well.

CONTENTS

ACKNOWLEDGMENTS

I am very grateful to all of my friends, staff, and church members who have encouraged me for over a decade to finally write a book! You never gave up on me.

Without the encouragement and support of my amazing wife Jackie, this book would not exist. Thank you for not only helping to bring this book into reality, but for building a wonderful life together!

I owe a special debt to my assistant, Jennifer Walters, who has not only helped to form the chapters, proofread every line, and worked with our publisher, but also lived through much of the content of this book.

Thank you also to my incredible Emmanuel Church staff team, without whom our church would be nothing. As John Maxwell has well said, "One is too small a number to achieve greatness."

—Danny Anderson

HOW DID I GET HERE?

Recently, I was sitting on my back porch with my wife and three young-adult children, having a meaningful discussion about some of the important things in life, like faith, relationships, and education. As we sat there, I began to think about how amazing the moment was. I looked at my beautiful wife of twenty-four years and thought to myself, *Wow, we are best friends who love spending time with each other and are totally excited about becoming empty-nesters in just about a week. Incredible!* (Our last child just left for college.)

I looked at my children, Andrew, 21, Beau, 19, and Ruby, 18, and thought, *These kids all love God, have a genuine relationship with Him, and are pursuing a life with Jesus at the center. Incredible!* In many ways, our children are normal, typical young adults. But in many ways, they are very different—wise beyond their years, investing their time in serving God, choosing good friends, and pursuing a Christian education at Liberty University, where I graduated and met my wife.

That night our conversation moved toward the church I pastor. We had just come off a four-night revival of sorts. Over fifty people were saved, and we did our first spontaneous baptism—177 people came forward to be baptized! It was wild! The kids attended each night and were very engaged. They had thoughts about the church and where to go from here. Good thoughts. I listened. It occurred to me that they like the church and have served in the church their entire lives. Even at Liberty, they still go to church without being told to go! Amazing!

The church I lead is called Emmanuel Church, and it is located in Central Indiana. I have been the lead pastor there for eighteen years. I became the lead pastor in 2006 after being the high school pastor for five years. Shortly after a very rocky transition (more on this later), the church struggled. Really struggled. Our attendance was more than cut in half along with our budget. I like to say that I successfully led the church from two thousand all the way to nine hundred. Pretty impressive! And I was only twenty-eight! Today, God has blessed the church with seven campuses, reaching eight thousand people weekly. We have a staff of close to 90 people and a budget of over ten million dollars a year. I still can't believe what God has done! More importantly, I still love God, my wife, and my kids, and I am more passionate about the church than I have ever been!

As we talked about the revival, specifically, what to do with all of the new believers and Christ followers who were baptized, my oldest said, "Dad, we need to develop some classes to disciple all these new people on the basics of the faith." I said, "Good idea." I did like the idea, but what I liked even more and what gave me great pleasure was his engagement. He has a heart for people. He cares. Many other things were said—and my heart was full.

I thought to myself, here I am with this amazing family—the back porch filled with love. Love for God, love for each other, and love for God's church. My heart was full to the brim with joy; no, it was overflowing with joy. What could I ever desire more than this? My answer was nothing. Nothing can compare. This was God's blessing to me. It was a sensation that neither a new car nor any amount of money could provide. No amount of fame could touch it. No experience of pleasure. It made me think of the last verse in Psalm 23, "Surely goodness and mercy shall follow me all the days of my life."

I thought to myself, *How did I get here?* How is it that I have so much goodness and blessing in my life? How did all of this happen? What has led to this moment? Now, to be clear, my experience as a pastor and father has been far from pain-free. There have been more difficulties and challenges than I can count. There is no family or church that does not have its share of problems and trials because, after all, families and churches are filled with broken people, and I am certainly one of them. I have been hurt deeply, and I have hurt others deeply. I have made my share of leadership mistakes, both in the church and in my home. But even through the mistakes, sins, and failures, God has been merciful. The question came back to me, "How did I get here?"

How in the world has our church and my family grown into something as beautiful as it is at this moment in time? These days it seems like all we ever hear about are pastors who are quitting or have fallen from grace. Pastors who have engaged in some sexual sin that has disqualified them. Maybe the abuse of power. Maybe the mismanagement of funds. Perhaps an addiction to alcohol or pills. We hear about marriages that have failed and breaches of integrity. After watching a recent Netflix documentary on one such pastor and church, it occurred to me that pastoring is extremely hazardous to one's health. The demands of the job are unrealistic at times. The expectations are beyond one's ability to meet. The attention can create an inflated ego. The speaking can wear you down. The difficulties of managing a team and budget are relentless. The challenge of maintaining a healthy private life with a very public life seems, well, impossible. The reality is that few pastors finish well.

Is it inevitable that we will burn out, fall from grace, and exit the ministry early? Is it inevitable that we will feel lonely, frustrated, and even angry? Is it inevitable that we will feel unsatisfied because our congregation isn't growing? Is it inevitable that the pastor's kids will struggle with the role of the church because of what it has done to their parent or parents?

I BELIEVE THAT YOU CAN LEAD YOUR CHURCH AND FAMILY IN SUCH A WAY THAT IT LEADS TO YOUR GROWING IN YOUR RELATIONSHIP WITH GOD, TO YOUR FAMILY LOVING GOD, AND TO YOUR CONGREGATION ADVANCING THE MISSION OF JESUS IN THIS WORLD.

As I reflect on my life at forty-six and my eighteen years as a lead pastor, I believe the answer is no! I believe that pastoring a church can be one of the most exhilarating, fulfilling experiences of your life. I believe you can and should grow your church and simultaneously create an extraordinary marriage along with great kids. I believe that you can lead your church and family in such a way that leads to you growing in your relationship with God, to your family loving God, and to your congregation advancing the mission of Jesus in this world. The reason I believe this is because, by God's grace and much intentional effort, we have done it. And continue to do it.

This book has been eighteen years in the making. I could not have written this any sooner because the verdict was still out. Would I make it? Would my marriage make it? Would my kids derail and walk away from faith? (Perhaps the verdict is still out.) I'm not done pastoring; however, I do feel that at this point in my life, it is time to share what I have learned with other pastors and leaders, especially as I see so many of them exiting early. I have attempted to put into writing a pathway to growing a healthy church without losing your soul. In these pages, you will discover principles and truths that will serve as a guide. Some I have learned from books and from observing others. Some I have learned the hard way, through trial and error.

My hope and prayer are that you will be able to glean some help, instruction, encouragement, and hope from the truths and stories I share, and that what you glean will help you to run your race well, fulfill all that God has called you to do, and finish strong! Blessings.

—Danny Anderson

Chapter 1

YOU NEED TO GROW YOUR CHURCH

Over the past few years, there have been some devastating stories of ministry leaders and pastors of influential churches who have disqualified themselves from ministry. These leaders were looked up to and admired by many. The consequences of their disqualification to the faith community were, and continue to be, confusion, heartache, and anger. Entire podcasts and books have been created to help diagnose and address what is going on.

The temptations and pitfalls that ministry leaders face are many and require much discernment, maturity, and wisdom; however, all this talk about pastors of larger congregations "falling from grace" seems to have had at least one negative effect on those of us who are still in the ministry and want to reach people with the gospel. It has made us gun-shy about growing the church. It seems that those who are evaluating the situation have identified the "cause" or "root" of the problem as having a large congregation or wanting to have a large congregation. The problem would seemingly go away if churches were content with being smaller and pastors just had less influence and power.

At least, this is how I felt as a pastor of a growing church. In fact, after reading one such book, I felt guilty for wanting to grow our church even bigger than it was. I began to question myself and shy away from any sermons on vision, growth, or evangelism. Big was bad. I'm sure I'm not the only pastor who has had people leave their church simply because we had become a big church. Suspicion was in the air. If you were big, you were guilty.

In the end, through much prayer, introspection, and counsel, I chose to push through these thoughts and feelings and listen to the testimony of Scripture and the Holy Spirit. There is no doubt that the challenges of a growing church are difficult and taxing on the body and soul, but that does not mean it is wrong or sinful to want to reach lots of people with the gospel; in fact, this book is written for the exact purpose of setting your ambition on fire and setting your mind free to do that very thing. My hope is that what I'm writing can serve as a "green light" for you to take the gospel to as many people as possible. After all, that is what we, the church, are for!

WHAT IS THE CHURCH FOR?

I believe with all my heart that the local church is the hope of the world. That was actually said by a pastor who disqualified himself from ministry some ten years ago; however, just because he "fell" does not mean what he said is invalid. He was, in fact, spot on. That same pastor said, "There is nothing like the local church when the local church is working right." Lost people find Christ. Bound people find freedom. Lonely people find community.

Confused people find answers. Broken people find healing. Those who have blown it find a second chance.

The church exploded on the scene two thousand years ago on the day of Pentecost. The first sermon ever preached in this new church produced miraculous results. Peter stood up with passion and conviction and told everyone to repent and believe in Jesus. Acts 2:41 tells us what happened next: "Those who believed what Peter said were baptized and added to the church that day—about 3,000 in all."

Three thousand people gave their hearts to Jesus in one day! Talk about a "big day" at church! This is incredible. In the next twenty-five years, the church would grow and multiply to 50,000 people!

From its beginning, the church was a growing, expanding, multiplying organism.

FROM ITS BEGINNING, THE CHURCH WAS A GROWING, EXPANDING, MULTIPLYING ORGANISM.

The church is not an organism that reaches a limit and then stops; in fact, that is a sure recipe for death. The average church in America closes its doors in forty years. Why? Because it stops reaching new people. It becomes a club. It becomes "member-driven" or rather "tither-driven." It becomes an insider-focused organization. Over time, it dies off because the people die off—literally.

Why am I taking the time to go over this? If you are going to grow your church, you must have conviction. Conviction is a deep belief that shapes behavior. Conviction means that you are convinced, deep in your mind and heart, that the purpose of the church is to reach the world. That's its mission, and as Jesus said, "The gates of hell shall not prevail against it" (Matthew 16:18). Without this conviction, you will find yourself giving in to the pressures of your critics, questioning yourself, or getting pulled into focusing on the needs of the people who are already there. You will spend 90% of your time doing weddings, funerals, attending events, counseling, Bible studies, and a hundred other things that people want you to be a part of. None of this activity is wrong, but it will not lead to church growth. Jesus came to reach the world!

Pastor, do a quick search of your heart. Isn't that why you became a pastor—to reach the lost? Have you lost this conviction? Has the fear of disappointing people or losing income taken over? Have the voices of the critics captured your attention more than the voice of God? Are you afraid that you, too, will disqualify yourself if you grow your church?

What we need most to push through the questions, doubts, and fears is *conviction*. We need a deep and abiding conviction in our souls that we are called by God to reach the lost people in our communities.

HOW DO YOU GROW CONVICTION?

People in your community desperately need your church. They need your church because their souls are thirsty, hope is waning, people lack meaning and purpose, suffer from loneliness, lack skill for living, and stand in need of grace.

Your church provides soul *satisfaction*.

YOUR CHURCH PROVIDES SOUL SATISFACTION.

The world is a hungry and thirsty place. It is a desperate place. The world is starving for attention, for satisfaction, for pleasure, and for a sense of belonging. The church is designed to meet these needs. In John 4, we meet a woman who represents all of us. She is at a well to draw water in the middle of the day.

Jesus shows up. He is there for her, but she is unaware. Jesus asks her for a drink, which was a social taboo due to her mixed nationality and gender. Naturally, she was confused by the request. Jesus pushes in and makes one of the most insightful statements in the Bible about the human condition:

> *"Anyone who drinks this water will soon become thirsty again. But those who drink the water I give will never be thirsty again. It becomes a fresh, bubbling spring within them, giving them eternal life." —John 4:13-14*

Human beings can find temporary satisfaction for their physical thirsts and cravings, but they will soon be thirsty again. And then they will have to come back for more. And they do return— to alcohol, porn, pills, gambling, video games, social media, and on and on. No matter what it is, we will always have to come back. As Solomon said, "Human desire is never satisfied" (Proverbs 27:20).

WHAT WE CANNOT DO, WHAT IT IS IMPOSSIBLE TO DO, IS TO SATISFY A SPIRITUAL THIRST WITH A PHYSICAL SUBSTANCE OR EXPERIENCE.

Jesus offers a "water" that will satisfy us in a different way. In a way that will allow us to stop coming back. Jesus says if we drink this water, we will "never thirst again." What could this mean? Dallas Willard explains in his book *Renovation of the Heart* that Jesus meant that this person would "no longer be driven by unsatisfied desire."[1] All people were created with physical thirsts and spiritual thirsts. What we cannot do, what it is impossible to do, is to satisfy a spiritual thirst with a physical substance or experience. C. S. Lewis points this out brilliantly in his book *Mere Christianity* when he writes, "If I find in myself a desire which no experience in this world can satisfy, the most probable explanation is that I was made for another world."[2]

Only a substance from another world can quench the thirst of a human being. Nothing else will do it. The church has that substance, the "Living Water." It is Christ Himself. It is the Holy Spirit. As people drink Him in, a bubbling stream of eternal life wells up inside them.

The woman doesn't understand what this water is. She thinks Jesus is talking about a special kind of physical water. So, He has to press on to help her understand. He must put His finger on her hurt. Her pain. So, He says, "Go and get your husband"

---

1 Dallas Willard, *Renovation of the Heart* (Colorado Springs, CO: NavPress, 2021).
2 C. S. Lewis, *Mere Christianity* (San Francisco, CA: HarperOne, 2009) 137.

(John 14:16). Slowly, the blinders begin to come off, and she realizes who has been talking to her, none other than the Living Water Himself. She is so overjoyed that she runs into town to tell everyone about the Messiah—all those people she was earlier trying to avoid!

You need to grow your church because your church has the Living Water. Your church is the spring that people need to come and drink and, upon drinking, find satisfaction for their souls.

There is nowhere else to get this water. It's either the Living Water, or it's a counterfeit.

YOU NEED TO GROW YOUR CHURCH BECAUSE PEOPLE NEED HOPE

The world is pretty hopeless right now. Everywhere we turn, we see war, corruption, violence, and hate. Social media has brought the worst of the world to the forefront of our lives every day. The news draws our attention to the most fear-producing stories. It's a struggle to be positive.

To lose hope is to stop believing in a better future. Hopelessness has settled in. Suicide is the eleventh leading cause of death right now in America.[3] Every year, forty-eight thousand people commit suicide.[4] That is 132 a day. Countless more struggle with depression, anxiety, and fear.

People are desperate for hope, and the gospel is the greatest source of hope in the world. In Romans 15, the apostle Paul prays this simple prayer for the Christians in Rome: "May the God of

3 Matthew F. Garnett and Sally C. Curtin, "Suicide Mortality in the United States, 2001–2021," Centers for Disease Control and Prevention, Centers for Disease Control and Prevention, 13 Apr. 2023, www.cdc.gov/nchs/products/databriefs/db464.htm#:~:text=In%202021%2C%20suicide%20was%20the,to%20premature%20mortality%20(1).
4 Mike Stobbe, "US Suicides Hit an All-Time High Last Year," *AP News*, 11 Aug. 2023, apnews.com/article/suicides-record-2022-guns-48511d74deb24d933e66cec1b6f2d545.

hope fill you with all joy and peace as you trust in him, so that you may *overflow with hope* by the power of the Holy Spirit."

God doesn't want us to simply have hope but to overflow with it! Hope is the deep belief that no matter how bad things are right now, they are going to get better. Paul says this source of hope is God Himself. As people learn to trust in Him, they are filled with joy, peace, and hope. It will overflow from their hearts and souls. People everywhere need this hope; therefore, people everywhere need your church. Their very lives depend on it!

HOPE IS THE DEEP BELIEF THAT NO MATTER HOW BAD THINGS ARE RIGHT NOW, THEY ARE GOING TO GET BETTER. PAUL SAYS THIS SOURCE OF HOPE IS GOD HIMSELF.

YOU NEED TO GROW YOUR CHURCH BECAUSE PEOPLE NEED PURPOSE AND MEANING

One of the most dreadful feelings in the world is the feeling of not having a purpose. Not having a reason to be alive. One of the most frequent questions I get as a pastor is, "How can I find my purpose?" Rick Warren's book *The Purpose Driven Life* has sold fifty million copies and has been translated into 137 languages. It is one of the best-selling nonfiction books in history! People are hungry to find purpose.

People need your church because God offers purpose for their lives. In Ephesians 2, Paul writes these powerful words, "For we are God's masterpiece. He has created us anew in Christ Jesus, so we can do the good things he planned for us long ago" (Ephesians 2:10).

What an astounding and insightful statement! God saves people to restore them to fellowship with Himself and get them on track to do all of the things He preplanned for them to accomplish. Have you ever wondered why He doesn't just take people to heaven after they pray to receive Christ? The reason is that through the church, people discover what their purpose is and are challenged and equipped to fulfill that purpose. This purpose gives their life meaning. People cannot thrive or even survive without meaning in their lives.

YOU NEED TO GROW YOUR CHURCH BECAUSE PEOPLE NEED INSTRUCTION IN LIVING

Living requires skill. It requires that we know how to deal with money. That we know how to deal with someone who has hurt us, wounded us, betrayed us, or insulted us. Life requires that we know how to handle stress and temptation. Life requires that we know how to build good relationships. Life requires that we develop self-discipline and integrity. We must learn how to manage our sexuality. On top of all of that, there is marriage and parenting. People must be good at a lot of things in order to experience a good life.

The world certainly offers advice on how to do these things. The problem is most of what the world tells people is terrible advice. I routinely shake my head at the advice spouted by people on YouTube and other platforms concerning sexuality, gender, dating, money, and success. My heart aches over the pain and brokenness I see that results from following the wrong advice being dished out by the world. Yours should, too!

THE CHURCH MUST GROW IF FOR NO OTHER REASON THAN TO COUNTER THE BAD ADVICE BEING DISHED OUT DAILY.

The church must grow if for no other reason than to counter the bad advice being dished out daily. The head of the church, Jesus, is the greatest teacher ever. I try to tell our church as often as possible that Jesus knows everything about everything. He is the smartest being in the universe.

The reason He knows everything is because He created it. He knows how it works. He knows how sexuality should be handled because He designed it. He knows it's better to forgive than to get revenge because He knows the damage that bitterness causes to the soul. When people follow the instructions of Jesus, they get better at living. That does not mean their lives will get easier necessarily, but they will get better. Better in the sense that they will find joy in pain. Peace in affliction. Strength in difficulty. Insight in confusion and wisdom for decisions. Jesus wants people to experience an abundant life, but that life must be built. Building such a life requires that people follow the instructions. He explained it like this: "Anyone who listens to my teaching and follows it is wise, like a person who builds a house on solid rock" (Matthew 7:24). Jesus would go on to say that when the storms of life come, and they will come, the house that is built through obeying the teachings would not fall. The contrary is also true. He states:

"But anyone who hears my teaching and doesn't obey it is foolish, like a person who builds a house on sand. When the rains and floods come and the winds beat against that house, it will collapse with a mighty crash." —Matthew 7:26-27

People need your church because they need a solid foundation. They need skill in living. They need someone not only to teach them but also to show them how it's done. Without this, they ruin their lives. It starts with you. Leadership author and speaker John Maxwell said it best: "We teach what we know, we reproduce who we are."[5] It is your example that matters most.

YOU NEED TO GROW YOUR CHURCH BECAUSE PEOPLE NEED COMMUNITY

The truth is that many people are lonely.

Statistics show that one in three people, or close to 33%, in the U.S. experience loneliness on a regular basis.[6] Loneliness is the feeling that you are by yourself. That no one cares. That you are on your own. That you are not needed. Loneliness is a dark place.

The most severe punishment prisoners receive, other than capital punishment, is solitary confinement. When in isolation for too long, the soul suffers. God created us to need human interaction.

5 Maxwell Leadership (@Maxwell_Leaders), "We teach what we know, we reproduce what we are," Twitter, July 26, 2021, 7:05 am, https://twitter.com/Maxwell_Leaders/status/1419614819657859074.
6 Michael Hunter, "Isolation Nation: The Startling Reality of Loneliness Hits 33% of Americans Every Week," *Medium*, 9 Feb. 2024, medium.com/beingwell/isolation-nation-the-startling-reality-of-loneliness-hits-33-of-americans-every-week-513ddcf5d99f.

When the church exploded on the scene two thousand years ago, we get a glimpse of what was happening in the book of Acts:

> *And all the believers met together in one place and shared everything they had. They sold their property and possessions and shared the money with those in need. They worshiped together at the Temple each day, met in homes for the Lord's Supper, and shared their meals with great joy and generosity. —Acts 2:44-46*

What jumps out to me in this passage is that they were together in large groups and in smaller groups in homes. Not only were they together, but they were helping each other, selling their possessions, and sharing with those in need. Mixed in was worship, joy, and eating. We can't forget that!

This is not prescriptive but descriptive. What we know is that the church met together often. And in those meetings, both large and small, there was love, joy, and giving.

WHAT WE KNOW IS THAT THE CHURCH MET TOGETHER OFTEN. AND IN THOSE MEETINGS, BOTH LARGE AND SMALL, THERE WAS LOVE, JOY, AND GIVING.

This is how people thrive. People need a place to belong. A place to give love and receive love. This is the church. Community provides the support people need and the encouragement people need. It also provides the accountability and instruction people need.

YOU NEED TO GROW YOUR CHURCH BECAUSE PEOPLE NEED GRACE

When you really stop to think about it, our world is a harsh place. There is not a lot of grace going around. If you don't perform at work, you get put on a performance plan. If you don't improve, you get let go. If you try out for the team and you're not good enough, you get cut. If you happen to view an unpopular political opinion, you get canceled. In a world screaming for more tolerance, there doesn't seem to be much tolerance.

The church is different. Our Leader is grace-embodied. John the Baptist said, "And the Word became flesh and dwelt among us, and we have seen his glory, glory as of the only Son from the Father, full of grace and truth" (John 1:14 ESV). Jesus offers people grace. Grace can be hard to talk about because, as Brennan Manning liked to say, grace is scandalous.[7] Grace gives second chances to people that our world and culture would say do not deserve second chances.

In John 8, some of the religious teachers brought a woman to Jesus who was caught in the act of adultery. They said to Jesus, "Teacher, this woman was caught in the act of adultery. The law of Moses says to stone her. What do you say?" (John 8:4-5). They were trying to get Him to go against what Moses said and have evidence that He was a heretic. Their plan failed. Jesus came back with this statement: "All right, but let the one who has never sinned throw the first stone!" (John 8:7).

7 Brennan Manning, *The Ragamuffin Gospel* (Colorado Springs, CO: Multnomah Books) 2015.

Immediately, they dropped their stones and one by one walked away. Why? Simply, every one of them had blown it. They were all sinners. We are all sinners. Not one of us is in a better position with God on our own. We stand in need of grace, and grace is what Jesus gave the woman. Grace is what we all need, and grace is what Jesus offers to everyone.

Pastor, have you experienced this grace yourself? Does it come through in your preaching and leading? Do your people feel talked down to or talked with? Are you deeply aware that God loves you and accepts you, not because you have cleaned up your act or grown the church, but because of the finished work of Jesus on the cross? Do you live and walk in your true identity that author Brennan Manning described as "Abba's child?"[8] If you do not live and breathe in grace, it will not come through to your people. You will, in the long run, relate to your people the way you understand and believe God relates to you. If they are to taste and experience grace, you must go first and live as God's beloved.

IF YOU DO NOT LIVE AND BREATHE IN GRACE, IT WILL NOT COME THROUGH TO YOUR PEOPLE.

The needs of the human being are many. They need satisfaction, hope, purpose, community, and grace. Without these things, people perish. They shrivel up and waste away. If people die without Christ, they will experience separation from God in hell. If they live without Christ, there will be "hell on earth," as

---

8 Brennan Manning, *The Ragamuffin Gospel*, 38.

the saying goes, in the way of broken relationships, addiction, anxiety, violence, hopelessness, and meaninglessness. God has placed you in the community you are in to push back the darkness. To bring people into the light. Your calling is the same as Peter's, who boldly proclaimed with conviction in his first sermon, "Save yourselves from this crooked generation!" (Acts 2:42).

The people who need these things are not far off in some other country. I mean, yes, they are, but your church is not called to reach them directly. There are thousands of people within a few miles of your church who need Christ. You are called to reach them. They are waiting for you to reach out to them. How long will they wait?

Chapter 2

SOUL CARE

Jesus said, "For what does it profit a man to gain the whole world and forfeit his soul?"
—Mark 8:36 (ESV)

In this passage, Jesus is warning people that trading their souls for power, money, pleasure, or success is not a bargain. It's not a good trade. To gain what the world says is "valuable" only to lose what is most valuable is a bad deal. I'm not telling you anything you don't already know as a pastor.

TO GAIN WHAT THE WORLD SAYS IS "VALUABLE" ONLY TO LOSE WHAT IS MOST VALUABLE IS A BAD DEAL.

Imagine for a moment that Jesus, instead of talking to a crowd of followers or would-be followers, is talking to pastors. Imagine you are at a pastors' conference, and Jesus is one of the keynote speakers. His words might come out something like this: "For what does it profit a pastor to build a huge church only to forfeit his soul?" That would be a bad deal. It wouldn't be worth it; however, as you and I have both observed in the recent past, that is exactly what many pastors have done in trying to grow their churches. Yes, we must grow the church, but not at the expense of our souls. In this chapter, we are going to explore what the soul is, how our souls become unhealthy, and what we can do to restore health back to our souls.

This is the most important work the pastor can do. We don't have to make the same mistakes others have made, and we don't have to allow the failures to cause us to shrink back from doing all we can do to reach people with the gospel. The first step in the process of "soul keeping," as author John Ortberg put it, is to understand what the soul is.[9] We cannot take care of something we do not understand.

WHAT IS THE SOUL?

I first learned about the soul from cartoons. I believe it was Tom and Jerry, to be exact. In one episode, Tom the cat dies (I can't remember how), but his translucent, ghost-like figure would rise from his body and fly. I remember thinking as a kid, *That's his soul.*

I was mostly right. Biblically, the soul is the real, tangible you. It is a combination of your mind, your emotions, and your will. It is the "you" that will live on after you die. I'm not sure if it looks like a ghost or if it's invisible. That part is not important. What is important is that it is just as real as the body it lives in.

---

9 John Ortberg, *Soul Keeping: Caring for the Most Important Part of You* (Grand Rapids, MI: Zondervan, 2014) 39.

The statement, "You don't have a soul. You are a soul. You have a body," sums up the human well.

Your soul can be compared to the engine of a car. It's not a perfect example, but it helps. The health of the engine determines the performance of the car. Like a car engine, your soul has a condition. It has been shaped and formed by many factors. The soul can be disturbed or distressed. The soul can be conflicted or at peace. The soul can be joyful or downcast. The soul can be content or dissatisfied—and on and on.

In the Scripture, the word "heart" is often used synonymously with soul. In Proverbs 4:23 (NIV), we read these words from King Solomon, "Above all else, guard your heart, for everything you do flows from it." Before any other guarding, we are to guard our inner being, our soul. Why? Solomon makes it clear that everything we do flows from it. The NLT says, "It (the soul) determines the course of your life." Wow! That's intense. What this means in our context as pastors and leaders is that we are to tend to the condition of our souls because it is the condition of our souls that determines how we will lead and the future of our church. Again, leadership and church growth are inside-out games.

LEADERSHIP AND CHURCH GROWTH ARE INSIDE-OUT GAMES.

To guard or tend to our soul, we must first understand it. I cannot take care of a car engine to save my life, because I do not know what its parts are and how they function. But I do know about the soul. Most of what I learned about the soul comes from Scripture and Dallas Willard who has written much about the soul extensively in his book *Renovation of the Heart*. He breaks the soul down into a few parts. We must learn what those parts are.

The Mind

The mind consists of our thoughts, ideas, memories, and imaginations. Our mind has a sort of condition of its own, having been trained to think in certain ways and patterns. Scientists say that 95% of our thoughts are repetitive.[10] Our mental condition has been formed through what we see (news, television, video) or listen to, our social context (friends, parents, associates, teachers), and books. There are reasons people think the way they think.

The Emotions

Emotions include our feelings, desires, and appetites. We say things like, "I feel tired," and "I feel hungry," and "I don't feel like going out tonight." Emotions are our feelings. Like the mind, our emotional state has a kind of default condition. It has been trained to want certain things and not want other things. To feel a certain way and not another way. Appetites have been developed over time by feeding those appetites. Certain emotions have become stronger and dominate by allowing those emotions to persist. Depression is one of those conditions. Although a depressed person can have moments of joy and happiness, they soon return to a state of sadness. Emotions are more powerful than thoughts because of their impact on the third part of the soul, the will.

10 Charlotte Mason, "Stuck on Negative Thinking," *Care Counseling: Minneapolis Therapists*, care-clinics.com/stuck-on-negative-thinking/#:~:text=According%20to%20the%20National%20 Science,%E2%80%94relationships%2C%20work%2C%20school. Accessed 22 Mar. 2024.

The Will

Our will, Willard says, is at the center of the soul. It is the place inside of us where we make our choices. From the will come our responses and actions. Most people, when they have a problem, want to focus here, but that is a mistake. Change at this level is only behavior modification. For real change to occur, we must go deeper. The reason it's a mistake is because the will is passive. It does not act alone. The will waits to receive input from the mind and the emotions, and only then does it have the information it needs to act. Willard explains it like this,

> *What we think, imagine, believe, or guess sets boundaries to what we can will or choose, and, therefore, to what we can create—our thoughts present a "lifescape" for our will and life as a whole. Within that "thought lifescape," we make our decisions that determine what we will do and who we will become.*[11]

He goes on to explain that he is the kind of person who will never rob a bank. The reason is not necessarily because he is a good person. That may be the case; however, the real reason is that he has never thought about robbing a bank. And because he isn't thinking about it, he doesn't desire it. Since he is neither thinking about it nor desiring it, it never happens. The mind, emotions, and will are all connected and must be seen as the whole of who you are, but change begins in the mind. Paul wrote, "Be transformed by the renewing of your mind" (Romans 12:2 NIV). So, the mind offers thoughts. Our emotions respond to those thoughts with either like or dislike. Our will gives in to the strongest emotions and appetites.

---

11 Dallas Willard, *Renovation of the Heart*, 96.

THE MIND, EMOTIONS, AND WILL ARE ALL CONNECTED AND MUST BE SEEN AS THE WHOLE OF WHO YOU ARE, BUT CHANGE BEGINS IN THE MIND.

Let me illustrate:

WE THINK –> WE FEEL –> WE ACT

There is much more to say and understand about the soul, but these three steps are enough for us to be able to understand how the soul malfunctions and how to care for it. Now that we understand it, let's dive into some of the wrong thinking that can trigger emotions that lead to actions that ultimately lead to a downfall.

As we work through these three major mistakes in thinking, I invite you to be honest with yourself. Ask yourself, "Does this describe me? Have I done this or am I currently doing this?" That is how we change—with honest evaluation and reflection. Here we go.

PERSONAL VALUE COMES FROM THE GROWTH OF THE CHURCH

Many of us are taught from a very young age that we are accepted if we perform well. It starts with our parents, who praise us when we do well in school, sports, or some other extracurricular activity. Coaches and teachers then pick it up from there. If we stand out, we get a spot on the team, or we get put in honors classes. After school, we enter the workforce, and our employers pick up the same theme. We get raises and promotions if we hit our numbers, and if we don't hit our numbers, we get stuck in a position, or even worse, we get fired.

This performance-based feedback makes its way deep down into the soul, and it becomes very easy for us to think of our relationship with God in these terms. God must be like our earthly father or our coach. Sometimes, it's not even God we are concerned about. It's our relationship with ourselves. Others have never felt good about us when we underperformed; therefore, we have never felt good about ourselves when we underperformed.

The result of this dynamic is that many pastors simply become driven. Driven to succeed. Driven to get results. Driven to win. Why? Because their value is at stake. Am I good enough? Well, that depends. How many people came on Sunday? How many were saved? How many joined a small group? How many were baptized? All of these are wonderful things, of course; however, when they are pursued for the wrong reasons, they threaten the health of our souls.

This has been a real struggle for me because when I was growing up, performance was the focus. Winning was the goal. My two older brothers and I played as many sports as time would allow. My father taught us how to play, and he expected us to be the best and to win. And we did win a lot. By the time I was twelve, our family filled an entire wall with trophies. (This was back in the day when you had to win to get a trophy.) Good performance was praised and rewarded. Bad performance was unacceptable. When you are raised this way and culture reinforces this pattern, it's a cycle that is hard to break, but we must learn to break it or suffer the consequences.

When pastors look to the church to answer the question of their value, what they are really doing is turning their churches into idols. The church becomes an idol that no one will ever find out about because they can cover their true motives with spiritual talk.

There is only one problem—idols never work. They can never answer the question of your value. There is always someone out there who will have bigger numbers, or someone who will make you feel like a failure or like you haven't even gotten started yet.

Looking for personal value in results will eventually steal your joy from ministry. Your heart will grow cold, and you will merely become a boss. You will be driven by an insatiable desire to find your value through the performance of the church. The result will be numbers, numbers, and more numbers. You will see your staff as a means to an end. Like others, you may get results, but you will leave a path of destruction in your wake. You will lose sight of the individual people on your staff and the individual people you are called to reach. Your heart will grow cold because all you are doing is running a spiritual business.

THE ISSUE IS NOT ABOUT MISSION, VISION, OR NUMBERS BECAUSE WE KNOW WE ARE CALLED TO REACH THE WORLD. THE ISSUE IS ABOUT *MOTIVE* AND WHAT IS IN THE HEART.

The hard thing here is that the church is about numbers. Numbers do matter because the numbers are people. The issue is not about mission, vision, or numbers because we know we are called to reach the world. The issue is about *motive* and what is in the heart.

The pendulum has swung too far for those who think the answer is to stop counting or to shrink back from growing the church. The real answer to the problem is to settle the issue of personal value and to do the soul work that is needed deep down. We must take our question of value to God, not the church. If we do this, we will set our ambition free to reach thousands, maybe millions of people, with the good news of Jesus. Our motive will be *joy* in people finding life in Jesus. We will be thrilled that God is glorified in the salvation of His people, and we will advance the kingdom with a pure heart.

Have you taken your question of value to God, or are you using your performance as a measuring tool? At this point, what do you see as your true motive for growing the church? Do you have some soul work to do?

RESULTS ARE ALL THAT MATTER

Many pastors would never admit to this thinking, but nevertheless, it's true. When results are all that matter, results are all that matter. When this happens, a pastor will slowly start to spend more and more time at the church. Most of the pastor's time is spent having meetings or counseling with people who need help. Time is filled meeting with the finance team, the leadership team, or the elder team. I am not implying that these meetings are not important; however, I know some pastors who are back at their church two or three nights a week, every single week!

But this type of focus produces other (not-so-fun) results. Family dinners are missed. Kids' games are missed, and so is any normal workout routine. The norm will be eating on the run. The other important things in life are neglected, and, over time, it will begin to show.

As this behavior pattern continues to develop in a pastor, anxiety and stress will begin to rise. Sleep will become more difficult, and since the workouts have been skipped, the pastor will begin to gain weight. A resentful spouse may emerge due to the pastor either not being home or rushing back to the church after a quick dinner.

Yet, as pastors, we justify it. How do I know? Because I did. We are talking about people needing Jesus, after all, and that is what I have been called to do! That requires sacrifice, and I am willing to pay the price. There was a time in my life when I had this thought toward my "less-dedicated" wife: *Didn't you know what you were getting yourself into when you married me?* What a fool I was! Thankfully, I "wised up" before it was too late!

Many pastors lose their marriage and family because of such thinking, but that is not the sacrifice that Jesus calls us to make.

Daniel was one of my coaching clients recently. We worked on a lot of things in the church, but our real success together came surrounding this issue. Daniel struggled with his priorities. Daniel was and still is a lead pastor of a growing church and is an incredible communicator of God's Word. His church was growing. There was just one problem. His wife and kids were paying the price. Daniel was working every day, often not getting home until 9:00 pm or later. When he was home, Daniel struggled to be present with his family. He had a hard time saying no to meetings. He felt like he had to be part of every decision. He tirelessly worked on his messages until they were "just right." I'll never forget the time he told me that he slept at the church on a Saturday night because he was revising the sermon for the morning. He told me it was Easter Sunday, and it had to be perfect. He stayed so long working on the talk, that it just didn't make sense to him to go home and sleep and shower. So, he stayed! I was shocked! I am still shocked!

If Daniel would have stayed on that course, I am positive he would not be in ministry today. His wife would have pulled the plug! Thankfully, we were able to get down to the root issues in his soul, gave him some good practices, and he made the course corrections. Now he is giving the appropriate attention to all the important areas of his life, and guess what? He is still in ministry, and his church is growing!

YES, MINISTRY IS HARD, AND THERE ARE MANY LONG NIGHTS; HOWEVER, THERE IS A WAY TO BALANCE THE DEMANDS ON YOUR TIME WHILE KEEPING YOUR OTHER COMMITMENTS HEALTHY IN THE PROCESS.

Yes, ministry is hard, and there are many long nights; however, there is a way to balance the demands on your time while keeping your other commitments healthy in the process. Pastor, are you giving your marriage the time it needs? How about your children? Are you present with them? How about your health?

PASTORS COPE WITH THE STRESS OF GROWTH IN AN UNHEALTHY, UNBIBLICAL WAY

This is where things can get really messy. Leading a growing church brings an enormous amount of stress. The more people you reach, the more problems you have! Stress seems to come at you from every direction. It can be stress about the sermon being good enough and connecting well with people, or it can be stress over an underperforming staff member who has been on staff so long that they are like family. If you fire them, you may lose not only the relationship with that staff member but also the relationships of three or four more staff and family members as well.

There can be stress over payroll and having enough money to pay the bills and mortgage. Stress about the numbers. Stress about sick people. Stress about a disgruntled member threatening to leave over the new lights you installed in the auditorium, the volume of the worship music, or the fact that the new worship leader moves around too much and sometimes wears a hat during worship! There may be stress over whether people are really being discipled in small groups or stress over how to get them in groups! Everywhere you turn, there are challenges that can cause stress!

How do we manage this stressful load? As pastors, I do not believe we are doing it very well at all. When I say we are not doing it well, what I mean is that we are coping with stress through some kind of escape. We don't know how to live with the stress, so we try to flee from it. This can take the form of substance abuse, alcohol, pills, or pornography—anything that will provide some form of relief. Sometimes pastors take this a step further by escaping into an affair, sometimes emotional and many times sexual.

When pastors fail to handle stress properly, the result is often anger. We get angry at the situation we cannot solve. Angry that people will not do what you want. Angry over incompetence. Angry over a lack of funds. Angry that you are not hitting your numbers. This anger will flow over and, in time, touch your staff and, eventually, your family.

Eventually, the combination of idolatry, wrong priorities, and poor, unhealthy coping skills will lead to some sort of failure that will disqualify you. If these things do not disqualify you, there is a high probability that they will lead to your quitting altogether.

Pastor, it doesn't have to be this way. You can grow your church without losing your soul. You can find your value in the proper place, and you can keep all your priorities straight and learn to cope with the stress of ministry in a proper, biblical way. Let's go there now.

GROWING YOUR CHURCH REQUIRES A HEALTHY SOUL

The hard truth is that the failure we have seen recently in the lives of pastors of growing churches is a failure at the soul level. Sexual sin is a soul issue. Abuse of power is a soul issue. Mismanagement of funds is a soul issue. Why? Everything you do flows from your soul. Every aspect of leadership flows from your soul. External failure is the result of internal failure to keep the soul healthy and conditioned. If a pastor "guards his heart" well and aligns with

God's will and God's ways, then his decisions and choices will be in alignment with His.

THE HARD TRUTH IS THAT THE FAILURE WE HAVE SEEN RECENTLY IN THE LIVES OF PASTORS OF GROWING CHURCHES IS A FAILURE AT THE SOUL LEVEL.

Let's push in more. Earlier I said that one of the major mistakes pastors make is trying to draw personal value from the growth of the church. This is destructive because it turns the church into an idol and a business. When your soul is healthy, you have taken the question of your value to God. You have looked at the truth of what He says about you, and those thoughts have penetrated deep enough for our emotions and feelings to be affected. First John 3:1 explains, "See how very much our Father loves us, for he calls us his children, and that is what we are!"

We receive His love and acceptance as adopted children. We feel His unconditional grace. When we fully develop this acceptance as God's child, it will eliminate all performance-based striving. The will acts with different motives, and your motive makes all the difference. Motive is what your people will be able to sense. Motive is what allows a team to trust. Motive is what creates a culture of leadership. Pure motives will build a team that is willing to take whatever actions are necessary to build a great church.

When we function out of pure motives, the church can continue to grow big and reach many people, but it will not feel like a business. Yes, there will always be business aspects to the church, but your team will sense the love in your heart for people.

Earlier, I mentioned that when results are all that matter, other priorities fall by the wayside. One such priority that will fall by the wayside is our connection with our spouse and children. The priority of our health will be let go, and friendships may even deteriorate. Our relationship with God can even take a back seat. This is the result of an unhealthy soul; however, when the soul is healthy, it finds a way to balance the priorities and put them in the proper order. When the mind discovers and absorbs the truth that if a pastor cannot run his home properly, then he cannot run the church, he will quickly put his family first. Paul asks this as a rhetorical question: "For if someone does not know how to manage his own household, how will he care for God's church?" (1 Timothy 3:5, ESV).

The pastor's household is his credibility; therefore, it is his priority. The marriage comes first. The kids' activities and games come first. Their feelings and thoughts come first. When the soul is healthy, the mind has affected the emotions in such a way that certain decisions are made that put your family first at the expense of the church. It is no longer something you do because you must but rather because you want to. Your family becomes your first ministry. Success with your family leads to success in other places, including the church.

SUCCESS WITH YOUR FAMILY LEADS TO SUCCESS IN OTHER PLACES, INCLUDING THE CHURCH.

I also mentioned coping with stress in a destructive, unbiblical way. The unhealthy soul looks for escape to "deal" with the stress. The healthy soul knows the invitation Jesus gives in Matthew 11:28-30:

> "Come to me, all of you who are weary and carry heavy burdens, and I will give you rest. Take my yoke upon you. Let me teach you, because I am humble and gentle at heart, and you will find rest for your souls. For my yoke is easy to bear, and the burden I give you is light."

Jesus offers to teach us how to live and carry heavy burdens. He offers to teach us how to live in a way that leads to the rest of the soul. This information has been received into the soul through the mind, and when fully embraced, the desire to turn to Him for relief will increase. Our thirst for Him will grow. The promise of rest will excite us. We will begin to make decisions to pursue Him and learn from Him how to live with all the pressures and stress of ministry instead of turning to alcohol and more Netflix to escape.

When you learn to handle the stresses of ministry in a healthy way, you will be able to stay in the game. The key to growing a strong, healthy church is longevity. To lead well for a long time, you must grow in your capacity to handle pain, rejection, setbacks, failures, and accusations. The only way to do this well is to walk in the rhythms of Jesus. That is to live the way He lived.

You might be thinking at this point, *Okay, that sounds right, but how do I do that?* Great question! Let's go there now.

If you want to build or rebuild a healthy soul, you must build healthy rhythms into your life. There are four of them:

1) Daily Quiet Time

If your soul is going to work the way it is supposed to, it needs to be in order. The most effective way to do this is by building the rhythm of a daily quiet time into your day. Pastor, you have probably preached sermons on this, but are you doing it? If you are doing it, are you doing it well?

The purpose of quiet time is to connect with God and allow Him to order your soul properly. What I mean is creating space to align your mind, emotions, and will with God and His will. That is the goal. The goal is not to get through a passage or even to read through the Bible in a year (although I do this every year and love it). The focus of the quiet time is to expose the mind to truth. To let that truth sink in and affect the emotions. To kindle desire. To awaken thirst. This takes time. Lots of time. The truth of Scripture must marinate in the mind. These days, my quiet time is at least an hour and many times more than that. Why? It takes time for the truth to stir the emotions of love and joy. Remember, emotions are powerful because they directly influence the will.

During our quiet time, we should ask, "God, what are you saying to me?" "What do you want me to know or understand about Yourself, myself, and others?" We ask, "God, how do things work?" "What is real?" We stay with those questions until God speaks to us. We embrace His voice, and we let Him move our hearts. Soon we become inspired and motivated. We have our instructions for the day, and we are ready to act on what we have heard Him say.

We enter our day this way, ready for action. Ready to lead. We make our choices and decisions based on truth and reality, and this will result in our acting in accordance with His will. This will play out in our lives throughout the day. We are patient in a frustrating situation. We listen more and talk less. We encourage those who are discouraged. We are kind to those who disagree with us. We rebuke and correct with love. We are quick to admit wrong and ask for forgiveness. We ask for advice on key decisions. Of course, no one does this perfectly. Over time, however, we will become closer and closer to the kind of leader Jesus would be if He were here in our place. This is guarding your heart, for out of your heart flows everything you do.

2) Weekly Sabbath

This rhythm is critical to the condition of your soul. It may even be more important than the daily quiet time for one main reason—time. A sabbath is a twenty-four-hour period during which no work is done. No counseling. No weddings. No emails. No phone calls. Nothing. Well, I don't mean you actually do nothing. You just don't do anything ministry-related.

This time is designed to give you time to dive deeper than your quiet time. It may include reading Scripture or prayer and journaling, but it is not limited to those activities. The main goal of sabbath is to let God be God in your life. This is why we stop working. The very act of ceasing from work is a discipline that teaches us that the work of the ministry is really God's. In fact, if you struggle to take your sabbath, I would argue that you have overvalued yourself and your importance tremendously.

The harder it is for a person to take a sabbath reveals an even greater need for it.

THE VERY ACT OF CEASING FROM WORK IS A DISCIPLINE THAT TEACHES US THAT THE WORK OF THE MINISTRY IS REALLY GOD'S.

Sabbath gives you time to take your proper place in your relationship with God and your proper place in the church. It teaches you that results are really on His shoulders, not ours. That He is the head of the church, not you. This is the essence of Psalm 46:10: "Be still, and know that I am God! I will be honored by every nation. I will be honored throughout the world."

Sabbath allows you the extra space needed to rethink everything. How you handled a difficult challenge the past week. Why you gave in to your flesh and sinned. Why you snapped at one of your team members. During a sabbath, we invite God into everything—our minds, our emotions, and our choices. We seek to discover why we feel the way we feel. Why we acted the way we acted. And then we ask Him to speak to those moments and feelings. We discover new ways to think about things, and therefore, new emotions and feelings are developed. We make progress because we are uninterrupted by ministry. We can stay with Him long enough to emerge differently.

Sabbath also gives us time to invest in the other priorities that matter. It is not a time to run errands and tie up loose ends. I take my sabbath on Friday, and it is typically made up of the following activities—an extended quiet time along with an extended workout. My wife and I spend extra time together on a date, often talking more than we have talked all week. I take long naps. Read long books. And have zero guilt about it.

During sabbath, we give our souls the attention and the repair they need. We go to God with all the stress and worry we are carrying. We go to God with the question of our value. We hear Him say again and again, "You are My child, My beloved." We invite Him in to heal the pain and the hurt. It is a time of healing and restoration.

When sabbath is done right, the end result is rest of soul, peace, and joy. Sabbath is a time to recenter your life around Jesus and to celebrate His goodness in your life. When sabbath is done right, it creates a condition of soul that you take out into the rest of the week. Sabbath is to spill over into the other six days, filling them with peace and joy and rest.

Sabbath is not just for you. It's for your entire team. I have had to work very hard to make sure our entire staff is practicing this discipline. You would think it would be easy, but some people just have a hard time turning things off. To help foster a culture of sabbath, we closed our office on Fridays. Our staff is not permitted to come in to work that day unless it's an emergency. This rule was communicated to my team: I absolutely care more about their souls than the results they are getting. It's hard to quantify the benefits of this discipline, but what I can say is that it helps our team function at a very high level without burning out and losing their souls. Pastor, if you don't model this and value it, your team will not either.

By far the greatest benefit of sabbath is teaching us how to work with God in our work. It is during sabbath that we learn to let God be God. What eventually crushes the soul and wears it out is trying to make things happen by yourself. This is not how we were designed to serve God.

The plan is for us to work with God in building the church. Listen to Paul describe this balance:

Him we proclaim, warning everyone and teaching everyone with all wisdom, that we may present everyone mature in Christ. For this I toil, struggling with all his energy that he powerfully works within me. —Colossians 1:28-29 (ESV)

We work hard and long hours, but we do it with a dependence on God. We learn to work in a way that is drawing strength from God's power. We work with the awareness that He is the one working in us and through us. This practice takes time to cultivate, but a sabbath will create the space for you to practice and get better.

Pastor, sabbath is not just a good idea. It's critical to your survival. It is the equivalent of taking your car in for a tune-up, oil change, and tire rotation. In the same way that negligence with car maintenance leads to a breakdown, negligence of the sabbath leads to a soul breakdown. Sabbath-keeping was the main idea that helped my friend Daniel to learn to prioritize his family and his health. At first, it was hard, like any new habit, but he stayed with it, and each month, we would talk about how it went and make the necessary adjustments. It was awkward for him to learn how to refrain from doing ministry for twenty-four hours, but now he finds himself relying on that period of rest to sustain him.

That is why God told us to do it. It is essential. Without it, you will lose your way. The soul will drift off course and look for relief in the wrong places. Attention will not be given to what matters most.

3) Quarterly Break

The quarterly break is essentially an extended sabbath. The goal is not just to take a break from ministry but to have extra space to allow God to have complete access to your soul. This break is the time to evaluate how you have lived the last ninety days. It's a time to look deeper into your motives and ask yourself if you are acting from a healthy place in your soul or from a need to find value and significance.

We cannot assume that we are "doing okay." We must carve out time to make sure that we are on track.

The quarterly break is a great time to read at a deeper level. Instead of reading a chapter of a book and then having to put it down because of other responsibilities, you can read an entire book in a weekend. It's a time of immersion. The soul needs this. Too often, we "tinker" with our soul, giving it a little attention here and there, but we never give it our full attention. You can get by with tinkering for a while, but eventually, things pile up, and problems occur. These things can include irregular anger, higher levels of anxiety, and more escapist behavior.

The soul needs a forty-eight – to seventy-two-hour check-up every ninety days. You will return with a refreshed, realigned inner being. You will think clearer and have more passion and energy to engage in the mission of the church.

Many pastors will think, *I don't have time for this.* I would argue the exact opposite. You can't afford not to do this. Remember, everything you do flows from your heart; therefore, the greatest gift you can give to your church is a healthy soul. Take the time. Do the quarterly break.

EVERYTHING YOU DO FLOWS FROM YOUR HEART; THEREFORE, THE GREATEST GIFT YOU CAN GIVE TO YOUR CHURCH IS A HEALTHY SOUL.

---

4) Yearly Vacation

The last rhythm I want to cover is the yearly vacation. Vacation sounds self-explanatory, but is it? I'm not so sure. I have a hunch that most pastors use their vacation as an escape from the problems and pressures of ministry. Relief is the goal. "Get me out of here" is the feeling.

I would suggest that the reason we use vacation this way is because the soul is in a bad place. You have not utilized the other rhythms to sustain health. You have neglected your soul, and now vacation seems to be the only answer. The soul is screaming for help, and the only thing you can give it is an escape for seven days. Many of us even leave God behind. He is not invited.

This will not work. I promise. Escape never works. The proper way to enter a vacation is to enter with your mind, emotions, and will in a good place. The other rhythms—quiet time, sabbath, and the quarterly break—will ensure this. Entering vacation with a healthy soul allows you to go even further with God. Instead of the time being used to repair what is damaged or reset what has gotten off base, we enjoy God for an extended time. We reap the benefits or compound interest of all our investments up to that point.

This is space for you to spend extended time in prayer and reading Scripture. It's a time to take long walks with your spouse, spending two or three hours at a dinner discussing all that God has done in the past year. My wife and I enjoy long conversations about what God has done in the lives of our children. (By the way, no kids are brought on a vacation. That would make it a trip, not a vacation.) This is space for you to discuss and pray about what God is calling you to do in the future. This is the time to dream. This is possible because you entered the time in a healthy place. Vacation should not be like a visit to the ER.

With that being said, an extended seven-day period away from the church does afford you the time to recenter on Christ and unpack some things that may have gotten "off." I personally treat my vacations as an extended sabbath. I go to rest my body and have fun with my wife, but I also go to meet with God and to hear His voice. I allow him to realign things inside. When you do this well, God restores your soul. You return to your church with an invigorated soul, and your staff will see a difference. You will preach differently, and the people will feel and sense the difference. Your impact will be greater because you are not acting alone. You are "struggling with *all His energy* that He powerfully works within you."

Pastor, the greatest gift you can give to your church is a healthy soul. When your soul is healthy, your motives are pure. Your team and your people will learn that they can trust you even when they disagree with you. You will lead better because anger will be absent or minimal. You will make better decisions because your ego will be in check. You will not be interested in being right but in getting it right. You will be a team player, which will encourage others to follow suit. Your value will be solidified in your identity in Christ, and you will naturally begin to prioritize the right things. You will cope with stress and pressure in the right way; therefore, you will not "lose your soul."

When your soul is healthy, you can dream big for the right reasons. Your ambition to reach people with the gospel will be set free because your conscience will no longer question your motives. When a marathon runner has put in the proper training for the race, he does not fear the race but rather looks forward to it. In the same way, when you put in the proper training of the soul, you no longer need to be afraid of big dreams.

WHEN YOU PUT IN THE PROPER TRAINING OF THE SOUL, YOU NO LONGER NEED TO BE AFRAID OF BIG DREAMS.

A mentor asked me one time, "If everyone followed your example, would they find life the way Jesus intended?" Wow! There was a time when I could not answer, "Yes," to that question. Thankfully, because I have implemented these practices, I can say, "Yes, follow my example, and you will find life."

Chapter 3

FAMILY

I love the church. I believe in the church. I want to grow my church, and I believe you do, too. The reasons are simple. When the church is doing its job, lost people are found, depressed people find hope, anxious people find peace, confused people find answers, lonely people find community, and broken people find healing. I believe the church is the greatest organization in the world, and it is worth giving your very best time and energy to. But never at the expense of your family. God never asks or demands that we prioritize His church over the closest people to us—our spouse and children. But so many of us do. This results in spouses feeling lonely and often left out. Children learn quickly what is most important to Dad and Mom. And in the long run, that choice—and it is a choice—leads to a breakdown in the home life. The Scriptures make it clear that we cannot lead the church if we don't lead well at home.

GOD NEVER ASKS OR DEMANDS THAT WE PRIORITIZE HIS CHURCH OVER THE CLOSEST PEOPLE TO US—OUR SPOUSE AND CHILDREN.

WHY DO SO MANY PASTORS PUT THE CHURCH FIRST?

There are many reasons. Here are a few that I witnessed and struggled with myself.

At Church, the Pastor Is Clearly in Charge

It seems at home, especially when the kids are young, things are always teetering on a state of anarchy! Okay, that's extreme; however, there is a built-in level of respect at the office that is not always present at home. At home, respect doesn't come from a title like Dad or Mom but rather through gentle, firm, and consistent leadership.

At Church, You Can Focus on the Things You Do Well

You receive regular feedback that your efforts in ministry are impactful and helpful. There is appreciation and even praise for the things you accomplish. At home, most of what you do is overlooked and maybe even underappreciated, if not by your spouse, definitely by your kids! All people, even pastors, want to spend time in a place that recognizes and appreciates their efforts.

At Church, You Can Work on Things That Move the Needle

The meetings you are having, the sermons you are preparing, the conversations you are engaging in all create an effect. You can often see tangible results, and you are helping people. You are helping people to understand God better, move forward in their faith, overcome fear and anxiety, or defeat a pornography addiction. *At home, it's often hard to see any kind of results that can compare.* When you have small kids, it seems like the goal is keeping them alive!

WITHOUT EVEN KNOWING IT, WE COME TO THE POINT WHERE WE WOULD RATHER BE AT THE CHURCH BECAUSE THAT'S WHERE WE CAN MOVE THINGS FORWARD.

Without even knowing it, we come to the point where we would rather be at the church because that's where we can move things forward. That is the place where we can be productive. This scenario is made worse when we haven't done the work in our soul to settle our value.

So, we spend more time at church at the expense of our families. Here is the dangerous part. Your family will put up with it for a while. They will even empathize with you because, after all, you are doing God's work. How can they complain too much about that?

Eventually, however, your absence, both physical and emotional, will exasperate them. The family will slowly lose patience. The excuses will stop working like they once did. Hurt will begin to set in after one too many missed games. Leaving to go back to the church yet another night for another meeting will cut to the heart. How many pastors' wives have said, "The church has become his mistress?"

In response to their pushback or frustration, we can tell our kids and spouses that we do love them; however, our actions betray our words. They simply stop believing us. Some pastors have recognized how important their physical presence is, so they do show up. They do go home for dinner. They do attend the events physically—but not emotionally. The mind is still somewhere else working on a problem behind the scenes. Putting thoughts together for a talk. Texting. Emailing. Emotionally disengaged. Your family will not be fooled by this either. They will know that you are there, but you're "not there."

Pastor, your first success is your family; therefore, they must be your priority. God has called you to lead them and disciple them before your church. They must get your very best, and they must get it first. The question is, what does that look like?

HOW DOES A PASTOR PUT HIS FAMILY FIRST WHILE ALSO GROWING HIS CHURCH?

Come to the Conviction That Everyone Is Leaving Except Your Family

It took me a while to come to this belief. Over time, it became obvious. There have been staff members, elders, and families in the church that I thought would NEVER leave my side, but I was wrong. They did. Not all of them, thankfully, but many. God called some of them away. Some of them made mistakes they could not recover from. At the end of the day, when things don't work out for a person, when the church stops meeting their needs, or they do something sinful, or the church goes in a direction they don't like, they will leave.

This scenario used to throw me off for weeks, sometimes months. It was the disappointment. The sense of betrayal. Now, however, I have come not only to accept it but also to empathize with it. I used to get angry and begin to withdraw from people, but that wasn't profitable. Things changed when I grew to learn that God is in charge of all that—where people go and what they do. He entrusts certain people to us for a while, and then they move on. That's just the way it is.

But not with my spouse or kids. They are staying. Staying because they are family. For my wife, it's "'til death do us part." We are in it to the end. With my kids, they are not welcome to stay in the house forever (unless they want to pay market rent), but they have my complete loyalty, and I have theirs. Even if you are doing ministry with some of your best friends, some of whom may have been with you from the start, remember there is a good chance they will leave; therefore, your spouse and kids get priority.

Very practically, this means that when they call, you pick up. It means that if there is a conflict with the calendar, your family wins. It means that they get preference.

See Your Family As Your Closest Teammates in Ministry

For some pastors, this one is easy because their spouse is on staff. My wife and I tried that many years ago in our ministry, and . . . let's just say that it didn't go so well. She likes me better as a husband than a boss. For some couples, it seems to work great, but I'm not talking about working together at the church. I'm talking about understanding the importance of having your family behind you.

When pastors prioritize the church over their families, the family begins to have negative feelings about the church. The church can quickly become the "bad guy" because it is taking Dad away from them. It is impossible for kids and a spouse to get excited about something that is removing you from the picture.

Pastors need their families behind them 100%. Great teammates assist each other, chip in, and provide encouragement. It is critical for the pastor's family to care deeply about the church and to feel as excited as you do. When they do, you will find the emotional support, love, understanding, and encouragement you need to make it over the long haul.

For that to happen, pastors must lead their families to see the church as a positive force. This means that you are present, both physically and emotionally, as I mentioned earlier. It means that when you get home, you are in a positive mood and ready to engage them in what they are doing. It means that they are hearing about all of the wonderful things that God is doing through the church in the community and around the world, and they see how much joy it is bringing you. This usually happens in conversation over dinner. Ask them what they think. Talk to them about what they are experiencing in the church, and listen. Even open things up for them to have a say in how to make things better. This gives them a sense of ownership and will create high engagement.

Whatever you do, do not make a habit of sharing the dark underbelly of the church, complaining to them about all the problems and frustrations, misbehaving staff members, sinful church members, and other church drama. Spare them this information. You don't want to put a bad taste in their mouths.

We made a decision many years ago not to talk about negative things going on in the church in front of the kids. We wanted them to love being at church and serving on the weekend. If you regularly moan and groan about the problems at church, and your family sees that the ministry is stressing you out, causing you to lose sleep, or triggering anger in you, there is no way for them to be excited. There are people to vent to, but your family is not one of them.

When There Is a Conflict in Scheduling, Your Family Wins

When it comes to church and family, there are regular scheduling conflicts. If you have kids and they do extracurricular activities, you will have to make choices no matter how well you plan.

When our kids were younger, they were involved in sports and choir. We made a clear decision that we would be present for them when they performed and competed. We did our best, but even then, I had to miss some things. This is going to happen. The key is to make it the exception, not the rule. If you are missing more than you are attending, the message becomes clear about what you value more.

This also includes family gatherings like birthday celebrations, graduations, weddings, and awards ceremonies. To be clear, these are not my favorite events to attend, but I know the value they have for my wife, kids, and extended family. When you miss these events regularly, the message is sent.

Schedule and Execute a Weekly Date Night With Your Spouse

The decision to prioritize our marriage has been, by far, the best decision we have ever made. We started when our kids were very small. We were strategic in finding some incredible babysitters we could trust. We didn't have much money, but somehow, we made it work. Many times, our date night consisted of some cheap food and coffee at Barnes and Noble. Many years ago, I heard a youth pastor say, "Dating is expensive. So is divorce court." That stuck with me.

THE HEALTH OF YOUR CHURCH WILL NOT EXCEED THE HEALTH OF YOUR MARRIAGE.

We still do our date nights to this day. Thankfully, we can now eat at some nicer places, and we don't have to pay babysitters anymore. The date night is critical because it gives you and your spouse the chance to engage in adult conversation. This may be the only adult conversation your wife has had in her day if she has been home with the kids. It gives you the chance to talk about things that need to be discussed without interruption. It communicates that the marriage relationship is the priority.

I would recommend that the date night happen on the night before your day off. This allows your mind to relax and leaves space for problem-solving and creativity. It's much easier to engage with your spouse when you know that you don't have to get up and go to work in the morning. The date night communicates value to your spouse and allows you the time needed to connect on an emotional level. The health of your church will not exceed the health of your marriage.

Take a Yearly Vacation Without the Children

I have often told our church that when you take your children with you on vacation, it is not a vacation. It's a trip. Trips are very different from vacations. I like to explain it like this: a trip is merely parenting in an unfamiliar location. Parenting is hard when you are at home. Parenting on the road is ... well ... *extra* hard. When you are not in your space, and you don't know where everything is, you can lose your mind. Does that sound like a vacation?

I will never forget one specific "trip" we took. We only had two kids at this point, and I believe we were in Florida somewhere. Our middle son, Beau, was about two years old when, one night, he woke up in the middle of the night with what I would come to find out later is called a "night terror." All I can remember is my son screaming in a way I had never heard him scream at 2:00 in the morning! I thought he was awake because his eyes were open. He wasn't. I held him and tried to console him to figure out what was wrong. I thought he was hurt in some way. He would not stop crying, and he would not listen to me, so I took him outside and just put him down. The sounds that were coming out of him made me think this poor child needed an exorcism! As he walked and screamed, I followed, not knowing what else to do. A few minutes later he seemed to wake up and stopped crying. As we put him back to bed, confused and exhausted, I thought to myself, *This is not a vacation.* No, it was not.

Now, don't get me wrong. We need trips. I encourage you to take trips. But vacations are different. Vacations are being alone with your spouse. Vacations are designed to help you relax and get away from the daily challenges of ministry and parenting. The two things that are distinctly absent on a vacation are children and ministry tasks. The whole point is to disconnect and be available to your spouse.

It is time for you and your spouse to talk deeply about important things. It is time for you to communicate that your spouse is number one behind Jesus. It is time to dream and plan for the future. It is time to discuss how life is going, review things, and make adjustments. Without a doubt, our best decisions have come either while we were on vacation or on the heels of a vacation because there is power in clearing your mind from all the clutter.

On one particular vacation, I remember discussing the amount of television our kids were watching and the content of the commercials. (This was before the iPad.) We didn't like the effect it was having on our kids. As we discussed it, we came to the decision that our children would only watch cartoons on the weekends. No television was to be watched during the week. This forced our kids to read more, get their homework done, and engage their minds in other ways. It dramatically reduced the amount of advertising our kids were viewing. The bottom line is to take a yearly vacation. Do the trips also, but never sacrifice the vacation.

Eat Your Meals Together As Much As Possible

One of our best family routines was to sit together and have dinner. Having this meal together is critical to the health of your family. Having dinner together communicates that the family unit is the top priority, not the individual family members. When everyone must make the effort to be there and be present, the message is sent to your family that the community is more important than the individual. The significance of the individuals is also validated at the same time if dinner time is done right. Each person learns to listen and respect all the other members of the family and, in return, is afforded that same respect.

Dinner with the family is time to discuss what we refer to as "highs and lows." Each member of the family was asked to share what their best and worst moments of the day were. Secondary questions were always asked, and that led to many meaningful conversations. This was our time to learn what was going on in the hearts and minds of our children. This is where we learned how they were feeling about things and how they were thinking about things. We learned what happened at school and practice.

This time would lead to incredible moments of laughter and silliness, many times crossing the line into craziness! There would also be times of tension, teaching, and correction.

When the kids were young, we were able to have dinner together four to five times a week. As they got older and started to get more involved in activities, it went down to about three nights a week. It's not possible to eat together every night. What matters is that you make it regular. By making it regular, you ensure that everyone understands the priority the family takes. You must lead the way in this. It communicates like nothing else that you care more about your wife and kids than the church.

Incorporate an Evening Bedtime Ritual

The first people you are called to lead spiritually are your family. God has charged you with discipling them before you disciple your congregation. The spiritual development of your spouse and children needs to be your top priority. You probably are aware of this and would agree completely; however, making that happen in reality is quite the challenge.

THE FIRST PEOPLE YOU ARE CALLED TO LEAD SPIRITUALLY ARE YOUR FAMILY. GOD HAS CHARGED YOU WITH DISCIPLING THEM BEFORE YOU DISCIPLE YOUR CONGREGATION.

The evening bedtime ritual was the most effective way my wife and I did this as parents. Almost every evening, when our kids were old enough, we would gather everyone in one of the bedrooms and sit in a circle with preselected Bible verses to discuss. One of the kids would read the verse, and we would talk about what it meant. Then I would explain to them why that particular passage was important to them and how it applied to their lives.

After we had a grasp on the meaning of the verse and its importance for everyday living, we would all attempt to memorize the verse. It's amazing how sharp kids' brains are when they are young. Then we would spend time in prayer together and head to bed. It was my favorite time of the day. I believe with all my heart that this nighttime ritual, more than anything else, shaped the souls of our children.

Control and Monitor All Media

Social media companies have made it their aim to completely capture your child's attention. All day. Every day. It is my personal opinion that platforms like Instagram, Snapchat, Twitter, TikTok, and others are more harmful than good. Children are not prepared to handle the dark dynamics of social media. It's eating them alive. It is your job to protect their minds, emotions, and wills (soul) from the dangers of social media.

The easiest way kids get access to social media is through a phone. My wife and I made the decision to hold off getting our kids' phones as long as possible. We made it all the way to their freshman year with all three. Even after they got their phones, we made another difficult decision. They were not allowed to have social media on their phones. This was a simple decision because I thought to myself, *What would it have done to my soul at sixteen if I had access to all of this trash?* The answer was simple. It would have destroyed my soul. While the decision was simple, it wasn't easy. Our children asked a lot. And we stood our ground. In the end, our children didn't start using Instagram until they were eighteen. My boys both recently told me they dropped their accounts. My daughter is eighteen as of this writing, and we told her she could get it if she wanted because she was in college, but she declined.

Somehow, amazingly, our kids made it through high school without social media. I can't help but think of all the pain, hurt, and constant comparison of themselves to others that we saved them from. If you think this position is a little over-the-top, just take the time to watch the Netflix documentary called *The Social Dilemma*.

When it came to the Internet and iPads, we did our best with the software that was available to us at the time. It was called The Circle. For about $100, we could monitor what was allowed to come into the house via the Internet. We could also shut the internet off each night, preventing any of them from getting on after we went to bed.

Keep the Conversation Going

Kids love to talk if adults are willing to listen. My wife is way better at this than I am; hence, the kids talk to her more than they talk to me. My conversation tends to revolve around what they need to be *doing* in their lives. Jackie likes to talk to them about what they are doing, how they are feeling, what movies they saw, how they did on their last test, do they have a crush on anyone . . . you get the point.

As I look back on our parenting years (not that they are over yet), it was our choice to talk a lot to our kids that gave us an advantage. The courage to have hard conversations. The self-control not to lose tempers. The desire and patience to understand, not just to be understood. The love to slow down and be gentle coupled with enough love to be stern yet kind. For sure, we (mostly me) messed this up many times, but we would bounce back the next day with an apology and hugs.

One parent may be stronger in conversation than the other, but this must be done as a team. We called it the "united front." Mom and Dad could not be divided because Mom and Dad talk about everything together. If the children feel like only one parent is doing the parenting, having the conversations, or handing out the discipline, there is a good chance they will jump all over that and use it to their advantage. There should not be a "private conversation" that Mom and Daughter or Father and Son are having without the other spouse involved.

That being said, try to talk about everything. Ask a ton of questions and really listen. Listen to what they are feeling about situations. Practice empathy. As you do that, you will earn their trust through love, and they will be more open to what you have to say in response.

HOW DOES ALL OF THIS HELP YOU TO GROW THE CHURCH?

That answer is simple. If you don't have peace in your home, there will be no peace at the church. If you cannot lead a small group of people (your wife and kids), how can you lead a large congregation of hundreds or thousands? Your proving ground is your family.

IF YOU DON'T HAVE PEACE IN YOUR HOME, THERE WILL BE NO PEACE AT THE CHURCH.

Paul explained it like this to Timothy:

> *He [the pastor] must manage his own family well, having children who respect and obey him. For if a man cannot manage his own household, how can he take care of God's church?* —1 Timothy 3:4-5

It's a rhetorical question. He cannot. The home of the pastor is the foundation of success. To be clear, it does not lead to success or create it. But without a well-ordered and peaceful home life, all of your efforts at church trying to reach people with the gospel will be built on sand. A few big storms, either at church or at home, and the whole thing will come crashing down. And the storms will come. I estimate one big one every five years or so. Will your foundation hold? Will you be ready? Are you prioritizing your family and making their spiritual growth your primary focus?

Chapter 4

LEADERSHIP

Now that we have sufficiently laid a solid foundation concerning your soul and your family, we can begin talking about how to practically grow your church. The answer is leadership. Leadership essentially has four functions. Leaders must cast a compelling vision, develop an effective strategy to fulfill that vision, build a strong team, and execute week in and week out. Along the way, leaders must solve all kinds of problems—some simple and some complex. It is only when a leader has effectively led himself, having done the internal work on the soul and properly invested in his family, that he or she is ready to face the challenges of leadership. Your mind is clear, and your heart is settled. Without the foundational work, a leader is building on shaky ground.

I love definitions. I try to give them as often as possible when I am speaking. They allow me to get my brain wrapped around what we are talking about. I believe it will help to first define what we mean by leadership. *Leadership is the task of gathering a group of people to accomplish an objective.* The story of Nehemiah is a great example. Nehemiah hears about the condition of Jerusalem, that its walls have been broken down and the city is in real trouble.

His heart is broken, and so he gets to work. He gathers a group of people, the Israelites, to help him with the objective of rebuilding the wall around Jerusalem to restore safety to the city and honor to God's name. Along the way, he faces difficult problems that he and the people must overcome. He is successful, and in fifty-two days, Nehemiah leads the people to rebuild the walls around Jerusalem. This is leadership at its finest.

A BIG REASON WHY SO MANY LEADERS STRUGGLE IS BECAUSE THEY DON'T FULLY UNDERSTAND THE FOUR CRITICAL FUNCTIONS OF LEADERSHIP.

A big reason why so many leaders struggle is because they don't fully understand the four critical functions of leadership. If a leader doesn't perform all four of these functions, the likelihood of the objectives being reached is slim.

FUNCTION 1: A CLEAR VISION MUST BE SET

The leader's first priority is to clarify what the objective is. What does the future look like? What are we trying to accomplish? Where is the church going and why? There is absolutely no other way for anyone to get behind you, support you, and sacrifice for the church if there is no clarity. A vision is essentially a clear picture of what the future will look like. It's the place you are trying to take the congregation. All great leaders are experts in vision. Perhaps nobody was better at casting vision than Martin Luther King, Jr., when he said these words in front of the Lincoln Memorial: "I have a dream that my four little children will one day live in a nation where they will not be judged by the color of their skin but by the content of their character."[12]

Nehemiah had a clear vision for the people of Israel. His message to Jerusalem's city officials was simple, "You know very well what trouble we are in. Jerusalem lies in ruins, and its gates have been destroyed by fire. Let us rebuild the wall of Jerusalem and end this disgrace!" (Nehemiah 2:17). Did you notice that he didn't just tell them what they were going to do, but he also told them why they needed to do it?

From the beginning, Jerusalem was to be a city on a hill, a light to the nations, and a testimony to the power and glory of God. For it to lie in ruins, its walls demolished, was a disgrace to the people of God and to the name of God. When Nehemiah said these words, he sparked something deep within his people.

As leaders, we often forget to talk about the "why." We may effectively focus on the "what" but still not get very far. It's because we haven't effectively communicated the reason why we need to do what we need to do. Without a compelling why, people will lack inspiration and motivation to follow and commit.

We know that Nehemiah's vision-casting worked because we find out in chapter four that within just a few weeks, the wall was already half built because "the people worked with all their heart" (Nehemiah 4:6, NIV). The people were all in. They wanted to restore glory to Jerusalem and glory to God's name!

12 "Read Martin Luther King Jr.'s 'I Have a Dream' Speech in Its Entirety," *NPR*, 16 Jan. 2023, www.npr.org/2010/01/18/122701268/i-have-a-dream-speech-in-its-entirety.

WOULDN'T IT BE NICE IF YOUR PEOPLE WORKED WITH ENTHUSIASM TO FULFILL THE VISION OF THE CHURCH? WELL, IT'S POSSIBLE IF YOU CAST A COMPELLING VISION.

Wouldn't it be nice if your people worked with enthusiasm to fulfill the vision of the church? Well, it's possible if you cast a compelling vision. The vision of our church is to reach 20,000 people on the weekend with the message of the gospel by 2035. The "why" is because we believe that without Jesus, people will perish. Not just in life after death but right now. We believe with all our hearts that to go through this life without Jesus means hell on earth. Jesus offers abundant life that cannot be found anywhere else. In Him is true joy, peace, fulfillment, and satisfaction. The "why" is clear.

Do your people know what the future looks like for your church? Can they articulate the vision to others? And do they know "why" or the reasons you want to take them there?

FUNCTION 2: AN EFFECTIVE STRATEGY MUST BE IMPLEMENTED

A strategy is simply a plan of action to achieve the vision. It's the how. How will you get there? Nehemiah had a strategy, and it worked perfectly. What I love about Nehemiah's strategy and what made it so successful was that everyone could get involved. When you think about it, rebuilding a wall around a city in fifty-two days is quite a feat. How did they get it done so fast? It says in chapter three that "Each one repaired the section immediately across from his own house" (Nehemiah 3:28). How simple the strategy was. Everyone was to rebuild the part of the wall in front of their house. Having been thoroughly inspired by an effective vision cast, the people went to work.

There are really two parts to an effective church-growth strategy. One is internal and the other external. The external strategy of a church is what the church as a whole will do and how it will do it; for example, the external strategy of our church is to reach twenty thousand people by 2035. We will do this by launching one campus a year for the next twelve years.

At the time of this writing, we have seven physical campuses with an online campus. The process of finding the locations for the next twelve campuses is not an exact science. We send groups of people out from the broadcast campus, send out letters, look for empty spaces, engage in conversations, and follow up with leads. We have done complete builds, mergers, and rented space in schools. This is our external strategy. It's a bit messy, but it works.

Second is our internal strategy or "what will each person do?" Each person at Emmanuel is challenged weekly to do four things: (1) invite their friends who are far from God to a service each weekend. At that service they will not only hear a relevant message, but they will also have the opportunity to place their faith in Jesus; (2) become part of a small group. We believe that spiritual growth happens best in the context of relationships; (3) support the vision with their time by serving on our *Impact Team* (serve team); and (4) support the vision with their finances by joining the *Kingdom Crew* (those who give 10% of their income).

It looks like this:
- Invite your friends.
- Join a small group.
- Serve on the impact team.
- Invest your financial resources.

If a good majority of our people are doing these four things (building the part of the wall in front of their house), then the vision is likely to be accomplished. People will not only be placing their faith in Christ, but they will also be growing in a relationship with Christ. We express our vision like this, "We exist to see people come to Christ and grow in Christ."

Do you have an external churchwide strategy? Do your people know what it is? How about your internal strategy? Is it simple? Can everyone engage in it? If they did, would the vision of the church be fulfilled?

FUNCTION 3: BUILD A STRONG TEAM

The first law of teamwork in John Maxwell's book *The 17 Laws of Teamwork* is the Law of Significance. It states, "One is too small a number to achieve greatness."[13] You can do many good things by yourself, but you cannot truly make an impact on this world by yourself. Why would I say that? The reason is because you have limitations. What you don't know far outweighs what you do know. The skills required to accomplish the vision far exceed the skills you currently have. You need a team, and you need a strong one. Without a strong team, you will hit a wall in productivity, and eventually, you will burn out.

---

13 John C. Maxwell, *The 17 Laws of Teamwork* (San Francisco, CA: HarperOne, 2013) 8.

Nehemiah knew that there was no way he could accomplish the objective of rebuilding the wall without the support of the leaders and the nation. After he inspects the wall for himself, his very next step is to speak to all of the priests and city officials to gain their buy-in. He simply cannot do this without them. They responded by saying, "Yes, let us rebuild the wall!" (Nehemiah 2:18).

A strong team is a team with strong players. The team I am referring to here is your leadership team, which is the team of people that you are leading the church with, not your staff. This group of people (three to five people) must be high-capacity people. Think of a championship basketball team. Each of the five players on the court has a different role, but they each perform that role at an exceptional level. Together, they win games.

These teammates of yours must be highly self-aware and secure in their identities. They must be able to think critically and handle a lot of pressure. They must be able to lead a team of people themselves. If they are not already leading a team of people, they will as the church grows. You must ensure that these people have done the internal work on the soul and have their family lives in order as well. A breakdown at this level is extra painful. My friend Shawn Lovejoy expressed it well in his book *Building a Killer Team*: "We don't just want more people on the team. We want the right people on the team."[14]

Your team must be strong in five key ways:

1. A Strong Team Communicates Effectively

As your church grows, it will get more complex. You will add staff, and entire new departments will be created. As time goes

---

14 Shawn Lovejoy, *Building a Killer Team* (Bahamas: Inspire Publishing, 2022).

on, each department will become a team itself, and there will be a tendency to forget that it is part of the whole. Communication will begin to break down. The leader's job is to ensure that information is flowing to all parties.

The best way to keep a healthy flow of communication is to systematize important communication. There must be simple ways that staff members and departments can share information. One of the ways we systematize communication is through our meeting structure. During our leadership meetings on Tuesdays, we have 10-15 minutes set aside for what we call "Good News and Headlines." This is anything that is going on that everyone needs to know about. This information is then passed down to the rest of the staff through department meetings. Those meetings also have time set aside for Good News and Headlines, and this continues from meeting to meeting.

Another way information is shared is through a weekly staff email that our executive team sends to everyone on staff. This email has important information from each department, and it informs the entire staff of staff changes, events, good news, and things coming up. Not all of the staff need to know all of the information, but the staff knows that they are responsible for any information that is conveyed in the weekly email.

2. A Strong Team Collaborates Well

A strong team works together. There is nothing more painful and exhausting for a leader than when two team members or two departments fail to work together well. This creates massive sideways energy. Instead of working on fulfilling the vision, you are working to help people to forgive, to overlook an offense, to not be so aggressive, to not be so selfish, to not be territorial or concerned about who gets the credit . . . and on and on it goes. It's enough to drive any leader crazy.

Because your team is made up of human beings, there will always be a level of this. You must do your best to elevate the value of collaboration all the time. The more your team members hear and see the importance of working together to get the best results, the less they will put themselves first, their departments first, and their feelings first. You will see more humility, more sacrifice, and more celebration when other team members and departments win.

A simple way I model this for our staff is to collaborate on my sermons. On a monthly basis, I meet with a group of staff to discuss future talks and series we are going to do. We meet for about an hour and a half to discuss possible ideas. Our media and marketing team is in that meeting as well to capture the main ideas to help create content.

In addition to this meeting, I meet weekly to preach my sermon to this team and afterward receive feedback on how to make it better. This meeting is on Wednesday morning each week. I then take their feedback and work on the parts that make sense for the weekend. These meetings not only help to make the talks I give more effective, but they also communicate that when we work together as a team, everything can be better.

3. A Strong Team Will Cover for One Another

This means that each team member will pick up the slack for each other. There will always be times when one team member is not on his or her game, or they may not even be present. Great teams have the ability to fill in the gaps and cover for team members who are down with a sickness, family struggle, or a much-needed day off or sabbatical. When one team member is not able to perform at their expected level, others join in to fill the gap. Each member of the team has bought into the vision so much that they will sacrifice for the team as a whole to win.

4. A Strong Team Develops and Integrates a Set of Values That Create a Healthy Culture

At Emmanuel, we call them our behavioral values because they shape and dictate the way we behave. Your values are the principles that will guide your team along the path of fulfilling the vision. Your values shape behavior, and behavior shapes culture.

Values –> Behavior –> Culture

For example, one of our values is excellence. Each team member knows that we will strive for work to be done in an excellent way because excellence inspires people and honors God. So, when a team member sees something that is done in an average, non-excellent way, they step in.

This creates and protects the culture. Your culture is essentially the "feel" of your organization. It includes the way people are treated, the way information is shared, and the way work gets done. When your values are clear, you can easily reinforce the good and helpful behaviors and eliminate or minimize the toxic behaviors. You can have a clear vision with compelling reasons with a simple strategy, but if your culture is toxic, things will fall apart. All four functions are necessary to vision fulfillment.

5. A Strong Team Gives Away Power

Strong leaders want to have a say in decision-making. If you or your leadership team wants to hold all the cards and make all the decisions, you will not attract strong leaders. You will instead attract followers and doers. To grow your church, more people need to be empowered to make more decisions.

This will require that you empower other leaders to lead. The pushback on this is and always will be, "But what if they don't do it right?" Well, they won't, at least at first. It's called growing pains. You must empower them and then come alongside them as they make decisions and course correct.

This is a struggle for most leaders because most leaders struggle to give up control. Giving up control is the price of growth. Giving up control requires that you let go of the idea that things will be done perfectly. You must let go of any desire to be seen as the one who "had the idea." You must let go of any desire to be seen as the one who is getting things done. You must be willing to share the credit.

MANY PASTORS BELIEVE THAT THEIR PEOPLE ARE NOT READY AND WILL MAKE MISTAKES. YES, AND YES. BUT, PASTOR, WERE YOU READY? DID YOU MAKE MISTAKES?

I can tell you from experience that the only reason our church has grown the way it has over the past decade is because I have been willing to let go of control. I have given other leaders space to lead and exercise their gifts. Craig Groeschel put it like this on his leadership podcast: "You can have growth, or you can have control, but you can't have both."[15] The pushback I get on this from pastors is that their people are not ready and they will make mistakes. Yes, and yes. But, Pastor, were you ready? Did you make mistakes?

When leaders do not empower other leaders, the good ones on your team will leave. The good leaders on your team want to exercise their leadership gifts. If they cannot do that, they will find somewhere else that they can.

But how do we know if they are ready for more influence and authority? Great question. The answer is simple. Give it to them; of course, give it to them in appropriate doses. As a rule, good leaders empower others when they can do the job 80% as well as they can do it themselves. Some leaders settle for even less of a percentage.

The best way to know if a leader in your organization can handle more is to give them more, watch how they do, and provide clear and consistent feedback. The good ones will flourish. Some will shock you. The process will be messy and difficult at times, but that is the price of growth. It's either empowerment or stagnation.

FUNCTION 4: EXECUTION

When it comes to executing the strategy, every church and organization struggles with something that Chris McChesney

---

15 Craig Groeschel (@craiggroeschel), "You can have control or you can have growth, but you can't have both," Twitter, June 17, 2017, 8:00 pm, https://twitter.com/craiggroeschel/status/872604100264951810?lang=en.

referred to in his book *The 4 Disciplines of Execution* as the "whirl-wind."[16] The whirlwind is the daily, weekly, and monthly oper-ations of the church. It includes things such as responding to emails, staff meetings, weddings, funerals, payroll, counseling, rehearsals, finance meetings, elder meetings, and on and on. The truth is that if you never set a clear vision and put together a set of behavioral values for your team, you would still be busy. Very busy.

That's the whirlwind. The whirlwind is not bad. It's just dis-tracting. Have you ever been part of a yearly goal-setting event that lasted for two days and got everyone all pumped up; how-ever, a few weeks later, all the excitement faded? Everything was back to normal. What happened? The whirlwind happened. It sucks you back in.

Strong teams build rhythms into the culture to stop this dynamic. In his book *Traction*, Gino Wickman instructs teams to create what he referred to as a "90-Day World." He writes, "The 90-day idea stems from a natural phenomenon—that human beings stumble, get off track, and lose focus roughly every 90 days."[17] To fight this tendency, the leadership team must create a system that helps to keep the focus on the objectives set for the organization.

Wickman explains that you and your team need to look ten years out into the future (vision). Then you should look at three years out, then one year, and then the next ninety days. What metrics would your church have to hit to reach your one-year goal? This would then give you traction toward your three-year

16 Chris McChesney, *The 4 Disciplines of Execution* (New York, NY: Simon and Schuster, 2021) 13.
17 Gino Wickman, *Traction* (Dallas, TX: BenBella, 2012) 177.

goal, which would put you on course for your ten-year vision. This discipline has been a game changer for our church's growth.

Let's say, for example, that at the end of three years, you and your leadership team decided that you wanted to average three thousand in attendance on the weekend. You are currently at 1,200 people. You would need to grow by 1,800 people in the next three years, or six hundred people a year. To grow six hundred people in one year, you would need to grow by 150 people in the next ninety days. Your team would then meet to come up with some "rocks" as Wickman calls them to hit that 150 mark.[18]

McChesney calls these "rocks" a different name. He calls them "lead measures."[19] He describes lead measures as any action that is both (1) predictive and (2) influenceable. By predictive, he means that this action can predict a change. When it comes to weight loss, the two predictive behaviors that come to mind quickly are reduction of calories and increased cardio exercise. There is enough data out there to know that these two activities, done together, work effectively to reduce weight.

By influenceable, he means that they are within your control. Meaning that they are actions you can take. They are within your influence. If you were a farmer trying to produce a good harvest, you could not list "rain" as a lead measure because, well, you cannot make it rain.

If you want to execute well and not allow the whirlwind to distract you and your team, you must create a 90-day rhythm with clear lead measures for your team. The only way to create these lead measures is for your team to meet before the next quarter

---

18 Gino Wickman, *Traction*, 11.
19 Chris McChesney, *The 4 Disciplines of Execution*, 55.

starts to discuss how you did in the last quarter and what lead measures you will commit to for the coming quarter.

IF YOU MUST DO ONE THING AND ONLY ONE THING AS A LEADER, DO YOUR WEEKLY LEADERSHIP MEETING.

You might be thinking, *Okay, but how do I keep track of all of this?* Great question. I want to talk to you about what I think is the most important action you can take to ensure that your church is healthy and executing the strategy. It is your weekly leadership meeting. If you must do one thing and only one thing as a leader, do this meeting. Four critical things happen in this meeting to ensure growth:

1) Relational connection. The first five to ten minutes are dedicated to good news that has occurred over the last week. This could be good news in the church or personal good news. This is a time to smile, laugh, and celebrate what God has done and is doing. The personal sharing allows all of your team to feel relationally connected to one another beyond ministry. This personal touch lets your team know that you are not just machines getting work done. You are human beings who have a real life outside of church.

2) Information flow. The next five to ten minutes are all about the headlines. This is time dedicated to sharing pertinent information that the rest of the team needs to be in the

know about. This is often information about staff, people in the church, or something that is going on in the community.

3) Accountability. If a team is going to execute well, there must be a rhythm of accountability built into the culture. This is accomplished through the leadership meeting by reviewing the previous week's to-do list and the scorecard. The to-do list is the list of action items that were agreed upon from the previous week. Each action item is "assigned" to a specific person, and they are accountable the following week for the completion of the item.

The scorecard is what you look at each week that tracks your numbers. The numbers that you track are up to you, but whatever you track should be connected to your 90-day rocks. This is how you keep your finger on the pulse of the church. This is how you hold team members accountable for the numbers they are responsible for. This is how you can see a trend in the wrong direction, and it helps you to fix a problem before it becomes a real problem.

4) Problem-solving. I mentioned at the beginning of the chapter that along the path of leadership, leaders must solve problems. It's the nature of the job, and it's constant. Nehemiah's situation was no different than ours. As he was leading the Israelites to rebuild the wall, he faced some serious problems from two men, Sanballat and Tobiah. They used threats and fear to try to stop the people from working on the wall.

Nehemiah stepped in and called a meeting with the people. He inspired them to fight for their homes and families, and then he came up with a plan that they would execute in order to defend themselves from a possible attack. The people kept on working in the face of real danger. Nehemiah solved the problem.

That is exactly what happens next in the leadership meeting. Wickman calls it the "issues" list.[20] This is a list of all the problems going on that need to be solved that week, usually four to eight issues weekly. This section of the meeting is the longest. It takes up to at least an hour of time. You lead the team to first identify what the root of the problem is, discuss possible solutions, and then push to solve it. This discipline of solving problems weekly in a systematic way ensures that issues do not pile up and become much bigger problems.

As a leader, you must perform these four functions well. If you do, you will build a church that is impacting the community in a significant way. Many lives will be touched with the good news of Jesus—and you will not self-destruct in the process.

---

20 Chris McChesney, *The 4 Disciplines of Execution*, 84.

Chapter 5

PERSEVERANCE

Years ago, I heard another pastor say that about every ten years, you will face a major problem in ministry that will push you to your limits and threaten your willingness and desire to continue on in ministry. I disagree with this statement—I believe it's more like every three years! Ministry is filled with problems, disappointments, and pain, most of which we are able to figure out and overcome without much difficulty. A key staff member may leave. There may be another shortage of financial resources. A small group may decide to become its own church. More empty positions that you cannot fill in children's ministry. There could be a person talking negatively about the church on social media . . . and on and on. All of us have these. No one is immune. And the bigger your church gets, the more this occurs.

These are problems that cause pain, no doubt. But then, there are the *real* problems. The big ones that cut deep. These are the types of problems that shake you to the core and cause you to doubt your abilities. When a staff member not only leaves but takes three other staff members with them and multiple key volunteers. When one staff member resigns and spreads negativity, and then three or four or seven more resign. When someone on your team commits adultery or develops an addiction to pills and starts stealing prescription drugs from other people. When you have to fire a long-time staff member because their position has outgrown their skill. When someone on your team sexually abuses someone underage. When you have taken out loans, and your offerings are not enough to cover the debt. When you launch a campus with huge financial investments, and you are forced to shut it down. These are examples of the "big ones" I'm talking about.

Here is the truth—your ability to handle these bigger problems will determine your level of longevity and success in ministry. This is the common denominator for all leaders of healthy, growing churches. Sam Chand clarifies the issue in his book *Leadership Pain* perfectly:

> *One thing that is common to all great leaders—it is not administration, it is not money, it is not staffing, it is not vision, it is not location, it is none of these things—it is their ability to handle pain . . . you will grow to the threshold of your pain.*[21]

Maybe you have never heard that before. I hadn't until I read his book. Think about yourself for a moment. How do you handle pain? How high is your threshold for difficulty? Can you process it quickly? Do you bounce back quickly? How long do you remain hurt? These are vital questions every pastor must ask. The answers to these questions will determine how far you will go. King Solomon explained it like this: "If you fail under pressure, your strength is too small" (Proverbs 24:14, NIV).

---

21 Sam Chand, *Leadership Pain* (Nashville, TN: Thomas Nelson, 2015) 200.

Eugene Peterson wasn't as kind in The Message: "If you fall to pieces in a crisis, there wasn't much to you in the first place." Ouch, that hurts!

If your ability to grow your church depends on your capacity to endure and persevere through struggles, how can we grow in that capacity? That is the question I want to answer in this chapter. Let's dive in. Here are five truths that can help build your capacity to endure pain:

1. PAIN MUST BE EMBRACED

If you want to grow in your capacity to endure pain, you must first learn to embrace it. Embracing pain is a mindset. It's a way to look at the difficulty. Most pastors look at the problems in their church as something they wish would just go away. And when they don't go away, they allow themselves to be discouraged, and I believe discouragement is one of the main causes of a pastor leaving the ministry. Even if one problem does go away, another one is sure to follow. Most pastors would love to lead their church and help people find Christ if their problems would just go away. This is just not realistic.

> MOST PASTORS WOULD LOVE TO LEAD THEIR CHURCH AND HELP PEOPLE FIND CHRIST IF THEIR PROBLEMS WOULD JUST GO AWAY. THIS IS JUST NOT REALISTIC.

What if you changed your perspective? What if you could learn how to incorporate the difficulties into the equation of growth? What if you could see the problems as a necessary part of the journey? The reason I suggest this is because it is true. Pain is part of the journey of growth. After a long journey of preaching and making disciples throughout Asia, Paul returned to Antioch to encourage the believers there. Acts 14:12 says, "They strengthened the believers. They encouraged them to continue in the faith, reminding them that we must suffer many hardships to enter the kingdom of God."

Sometimes we just need to be reminded that pain and suffering are par for the course. When Jesus chose Saul to be His vessel to bring the gospel to the Gentiles, He chose him to suffer. In Acts 9:15-16, Jesus made this comment to Ananias: "Go, for Saul is my chosen instrument to take my message to the Gentiles and to kings, as well as to the people of Israel. And I will show him how much he must suffer for my name's sake." Paul would go on to suffer unimaginable pain—being whipped, stoned, beaten, hungry, homeless, and freezing—all for the sake of the gospel. His threshold for pain was through the roof. No wonder God used him to get Christianity off the ground!

Embracing the pain means that you have mentally and emotionally accepted the pain. It means that you are not just grunting through it, but rather you see it as God's will for your life. You receive it as something God is doing and allowing because, in fact, He is. When we can come to see pain in leadership as sovereignly ordained or allowed by our Father in heaven, we can rest assured that He has a purpose in it. We come to trust that "God causes everything to work together for the good of those who love God and are called according to his purpose for them" (Romans 8:28). This assurance allows the peace of God to fill our lives as we go through the pain. We can come to trust the heart of God as Job ultimately did at the end of his struggles. On the other hand, when you and I resent and resist problems, we are resenting the will of God. This leads to bitterness, anger, and discouragement. If you want to grow in your capacity to endure pain, you must fully accept it as part of the journey of growth.

2. SOME THINGS CAN ONLY BE LEARNED THROUGH PAIN

It pains me to say this, but there are some lessons that can *only* be learned through difficulty. Lessons about yourself, other people, and God are examples. I love to learn. I read books like crazy. I go to conferences and listen to podcasts all the time. You probably do, too. That is your responsibility as a leader. Leaders are learners (more on this in the next chapter). We can learn so much from the content produced by others, but there are the things you can only learn because you have felt them deeply within your soul. You have cried the tears and lost the sleep and felt the fear. You have tasted the bitter flavor of betrayal and felt the sensation of being all alone. Books and podcasts cannot put you into that place of discovery. Pain forces us to take a hard look at ourselves and deal with what we find. It places us in a position where we must actually trust in God and deal with our inadequacies and fears.

Back in 2006, the founding pastor of our church decided to retire. The church almost unanimously voted for me to be his replacement. From that high point, things went south quickly. I was a different kind of leader. I didn't wear suits and didn't like choir music. I didn't like teal carpet or chandeliers in the sanctuary. To make a long story short, people didn't like me. So, they left. Lots of them.

IT PAINS ME TO SAY THIS, BUT THERE ARE SOME LESSONS THAT CAN ONLY BE LEARNED THROUGH DIFFICULTY.

The church went from two thousand in attendance down to nine hundred in about eight months or so. Stellar leadership on my part. Our offerings went from $70,000 a week to just under $30,000. We had to let seven staff members go to stay in the black. Even then, we almost didn't make it. Every week, I would hear about a new family that had left.

For almost two full years, our team tried everything to keep things from falling apart. I preached as hard as I could, talked about the vision as much as I could, answered questions, and had many two– to three-hour meetings with disgruntled church members, none of which resulted in their staying. For many months, I thought I could figure it out with the right actions and strategies.

Finally, I surrendered total control of the situation to God. I was done. I remember praying something like this, "Lord, I'm out of ideas. I've got nothing left. If you want this church to survive, you are going to have to save it. I give up. It's up to you." It was sometime in 2007 when I truly put all of my hope in God and came to the end of my rope.

It wasn't long after that moment that our financial person informed me of the date that we would be out of money. She had a graph that showed the actual date! I said to myself, *Okay, there it is. That's when we all will have to go get jobs because there is no money for payroll.*

About a week later, after a sermon, a man I had never met came down front and told me he wanted to help. After a short inquiry, he handed me a blank check. I was confused. He said, "Write the number down that you need in order to make it through this downturn." I didn't believe him, so I asked if we could set up a meeting the following day so that I could understand what he was saying. He showed up the next day and told me the same thing. I asked our team what we needed to pay the bills, and they told me $25,000. That is what I wrote on the check. It cleared, and we paid our bills that month!

I had told God I was done, and that's when He showed up. It was in this dark place of feeling like a failure and questioning my calling that God taught me I could really trust Him. God was big enough to handle our problems. It was this experience that taught me to trust God in a way I never had before. The only mistake I made that day was not putting an extra zero on that check! Darn It!

EVENTUALLY, GOD MUST BRING YOU TO THE POINT WHERE YOU STOP RELYING ON YOURSELF.

Pastor, eventually, God must bring you to the point where you stop relying on yourself. This lesson requires extreme pain. You are stubborn and deeply self-reliant. Don't worry; this was Paul's problem too. He describes his situation in 2 Corinthians 1:8-9:

> *We were crushed and overwhelmed beyond our ability to endure, and we thought we would never live through it. In fact, we expected to die. But as a result, we stopped relying on ourselves and learned to rely on God, who raises the dead.*

Wow! Even the great apostle Paul had to learn things through pain. Dallas Willard was fond of saying, "God's address is the end of your rope."[22]

3. INVITE OTHERS INTO THE PAIN

It is hard as the leader to be vulnerable with your team or with a small group, but we must avoid this tendency and let others in. We struggle to open up because we think that we will look weak in front of our peers. This is certainly true if we make it a regular practice. Our team will lack confidence in us and will struggle to follow our leadership; however, on those rare occasions when the pain is severe, we must push ourselves to be vulnerable.

The reason we must be vulnerable in our times of pain is simple. They will help you. Your team or small group can provide strength for you to endure. They will pray for you. They will bear the burden and carry the load with you. Even more, they will give you valuable insight and perspective. Solomon explained it to us like this, "If one person falls, the other can reach out and help. But someone who falls alone is in real trouble" (Ecclesiastes 4:10).

---

22 Sean Meade, "Dallas Notes: Theology Conference 2009: Life in the Spirit (Wheaton, April 17, 2009)," *The Wisdom of Dallas Willard*, 26 Jan. 2014, thewisdomofdallaswillard.blogspot.com/2014/01/dallas-notes-theology-conference-2009.html.

When you choose to go through pain alone, you forfeit the help God has prepared to give you through others. A few years ago, during the pandemic, many churches suffered severe pain. If COVID-19 wasn't enough, every church had to navigate the social unrest after George Floyd died. Many churches suffered. Ours was no different. Our pain was mostly internal at the staff level. We had seven staff members resign in a short amount of time. The reasons they gave were mostly because of my leadership and the positions I was taking on issues during that time. Accusations were officially made to our elders, and things got serious quickly.

PASTOR, IT IS NOT A GOOD IDEA TO HIDE YOUR PAIN AND TRY TO GO THROUGH IT ALONE. IF YOU DON'T WANT TO OPEN UP TO YOUR STAFF, AT LEAST FIND A GOOD CHRISTIAN COUNSELOR TO TALK WITH. YOU ARE NOT WIRED TO DEAL WITH HURT BY YOURSELF.

Everything inside of me wanted to retreat and hide. I wanted to ignore the pain of the accusations, put my head down, and just keep moving and maybe deal with it later. Thankfully, I didn't choose to take that path. I opened up to my team and shared my heart. They opened up to me, and we shared the burden together. For months, we walked together through the difficulty. I opened up to our elders and worked together with them to address the concerns that our former staff members had. Yes, it was an extremely difficult time, but I didn't have to go through it alone. In the end, we all learned that we can count on each other when times get hard.

Pastor, it is not a good idea to hide your pain and try to go through it alone. If you don't want to open up to your staff, at least find a good Christian counselor to talk with. You are not wired to deal with hurt by yourself.

4. THE PAIN ALWAYS PRESENTS AN OPPORTUNITY

In Matthew 10:8, Jesus is sending out His disciples to preach and do ministry. He empowers them with great authority to "Heal the sick, raise the dead, cure those with leprosy, and cast out demons." Pretty cool stuff. They must have been pumped, especially the part about raising the dead!

But then Jesus says something else that probably caused them to lose a bit of their enthusiasm. He says, "But beware! For you will be handed over to the courts and will be flogged with whips in the synagogues. You will stand trial before governors and kings because you are my followers" (Matthew 10:17-18a). Wait, flogged with whips? Are you serious? I wish I were there to see their faces. If I had been there, I might have excused myself from the team.

How does Jesus help them with their human emotions of fear? He tells them, "But this will be your opportunity to tell the rulers and other unbelievers about me" (Matthew 10:18b). This probably didn't chase away their fears entirely, but it did give them purpose. Where there is purpose, there is meaning. Their pain would present an opportunity to speak the message of eternal life to people who needed to hear it.

When pain hits, ask yourself, "Where is the opportunity?" Difficulty and struggle are clear opportunities for you to become resourceful. When you have less to work with, you must become creative. When you have less staff, it's an opportunity to get better at developing volunteers. When you have less money, it's an opportunity to get better at developing givers. When you have less time, it's an opportunity to reprioritize what you are doing.

Perhaps no one explained this better than Ryan Holiday in his book *The Obstacle Is the Way* when he wrote, "The obstacle in the path becomes the path. Never forget, within every obstacle is an opportunity to improve our condition."[23] It's true that God never wastes a hurt. Before COVID-19 hit, our church was breaking records. In 2018, we were named the fourth fastest-growing church in the nation, according to *Outreach Magazine*. It seemed like everything was working in our favor.

Then, the shutdown came, and in the blink of an eye, our doors—most likely just like yours—were closed. All momentum was lost. Everything we had worked for seemed like it was gone in an instant. Apart from our transition back in 2006-2008, this was the hardest challenge we had ever had to face. It was the closest I had ever come to being depressed. I moped around for what seemed like weeks. I lost my passion and enthusiasm. I cannot remember how long it lasted, but it seemed like an eternity!

Slowly, however, something started to change in me. Our team began to ask the questions, "Where is the opportunity here?" "What can we learn?" and "Where can we get better?" It soon became clear that, although we had a decent online experience for our church pre-COVID-19, it needed to be better. That was

---

23   Ryan Holiday, *The Obstacle Is the Way* (New York, NY: Penguin, 2014) 7.

it! This was our chance to pour money and effort into making the online experience top-of-the-line.

Our team went to work. We quickly turned our auditorium into a studio. We added cameras. I learned how to speak directly to the camera, a skill I had previously struggled with. We informed our congregation it was business as usual, just all online. We made it even more clear on how to give, which stabilized our income through the entire pandemic. (This was a shift that we are still seeing the positive effects of today.) We hired a full-time online campus pastor and took our online platform from being a place to watch sermons to a place that people could call "their church."

I am not in love with the idea of online church. It has limitations, but the evidence is clear that it is effective if done well. Today, we don't have an online service to watch; we have an online campus to experience. It's our second-largest gathering on the weekend, and we continue to see people come to Christ and grow in Christ online. We have found that often our online campus is our front door, where people can "try out" our church before walking into one of our physical locations. All of this came from the decision to look for the opportunity in the pain that COVID-19 presented us.

Pastor, if you want to grow your church, you must look for the opportunity in the pain. It is there because God never wastes a hurt. Are you looking for it? Take a moment right now and evaluate the pain you are currently in. Where is the opportunity? Is it an opportunity for you to be a better leader? Create a healthier culture? Recruit a new staff member? Make your assimilation process better? Look for the opportunity because I promise you—it's there.

5. THE PAIN IS PART OF THE GROWTH

This last truth that can help build your capacity to endure pain is all about perspective. Perspective is the way you look at things or the way you interpret events. If you are a parent, you know how important perspective is. Most of parenting is about adjusting your kids' perspectives on things.

How do they view a situation when a friend has left them out? How do they understand the dangers of social media and why you're not allowing them to have it? How do they view the importance of homework and studying? How do they view the effort needed to succeed at a sport? How do they look at the importance of choosing good friends and on and on? Our best parenting was done when we could help our kids have the proper perspectives on the events and issues going on in their lives.

How we interpret events determines how we feel about them and what we will do next. One of the greatest choices you can make as a pastor and leader is to interpret pain of all kinds as positive because it leads to growth. This takes a lot of work because as I have said in an earlier chapter, we are emotional creatures, and pain is emotional.

Developing the ability to have this perspective on pain requires a lot of mental work. Two passages of scripture have been critical for me in developing this discipline. They are James 1:2-4 and Romans 5:3-5. First, let's look at James:

> *Dear brothers and sisters, when troubles of any kind come your way, consider it an opportunity for great joy. For you know that when your faith is tested, your endurance has a chance to grow. So let it grow, for when your endurance is fully developed, you will be perfect and complete, needing nothing.*

What a truth! Pain and difficulty are opportunities for endurance to grow. How ironic. The very thing we want to avoid—pain—is what we need to build the inner strength to persevere. That's why pain is an "opportunity for great joy." When God allows pain, He is growing you into the leader He needs you to be. It's not time to be discouraged or resentful. It's time to rejoice!

This is exactly how Paul expresses it in Romans 5:3-5:

We can rejoice, too, when we run into problems and trials, for we know that they help us develop endurance. And endurance develops strength of character, and character strengthens our confident hope of salvation. And this hope will not lead to disappointment.

Incredible! Problems and trials not only develop endurance but also a strong character that leads to confident hope. Hope is no small thing. Hope is real inner strength to keep moving forward because hope says things are going to be better in the future. Hope is an emotion and a conviction that God is at work preparing you for a brighter future.

This is the proper perspective of pain. The reality is that your pain can make you bitter or it can make you better. What makes the difference is your perspective. The good news is that you get to choose your perspective. You have complete freedom to give meaning to the painful events that take place in your life.

The reality is that you will face pain in one form or another every single week. Jerry Falwell, the founder of Liberty University, was fond of saying, "There are never two good days in a row in ministry." If your church is like mine, there are marriages coming to an end, abusive situations people are trying to get out of, suicides, internal conflict between staff members, a shortage of resources, and a shortage of volunteers. Angela Duckworth has written a fantastic book called *Grit*. One of the questions she seeks to answer through her research is how certain people can endure through difficulty and pain. She discovered that one of the main reasons that some people can push forward while others tend to give up is the way they interpret setbacks. She writes, "Overwhelmingly, I've found that they [gritty people] explain events optimistically."[24] We all explain events to ourselves. We tell a story to ourselves and others about what things mean. That story can be positive or negative.

PASTOR, IF YOU WANT TO GROW YOUR CHURCH AND REACH PEOPLE WITH THE GOSPEL, THERE IS PAIN AHEAD. BUT THE PAIN HAS A PURPOSE—YOUR GROWTH.

Ryan Holiday explained this very clearly when he wrote, "Seen properly, everything that happens—be it an economic crash or a personal tragedy—is a chance to move forward."[25] Pastor, if you want to grow your church and reach people with the gospel, there is pain ahead. But the pain has a purpose—your growth. If you can begin to see the pain in this light, you will train yourself to accept it instead of resenting it. If you resent the pain, you will become bitter and angry at people and maybe even God. If

---

24   Angela Duckworth, *Grit: The Power of Passion and Perseverance* (New York, NY: Scribner, 2016) 175.
25   Ryan Holiday, *The Obstacle Is the Way*, 18.

you allow pain and resentment to settle into your soul, it's just a matter of time before you are looking for a way out. People call it "church hurt." The only way to block the enemy from trapping you in this way is to see it differently. You must embrace the pain as part of the process of growth—both your personal growth and the growth of the church. No pain, no gain. As Sam Chand stated, at the end of the day, "The growth of your church depends on your ability to grow in your capacity to endure pain."

How big is your capacity to endure pain? Have you learned to embrace the pain? Have you invited others into the pain? Are you looking for the opportunity in the pain? Have you developed the proper perspective on pain?

Chapter 6

COMMIT TO CONTINUOUS IMPROVEMENT

Believe it or not, there was a time when Michael Jordan was not the best basketball player in the world. He was a freshman in college. According to his teammates and coaches, he was inconsistent, not a great ball handler, and his jump shot was sketchy; however, Dean Smith, his coach at North Carolina, would later say about Michael, "…He was one of the most competitive ones we ever had in our drills. He wanted to get better and had the ability to get better."[26] And he did get better, a lot better. He would carry that same mentality and commitment to become the best basketball player throughout his entire career, which has earned him the spot of being the GOAT (Greatest Of All Time). (If you disagree, you are delusional and need pastoral care.)

Growth requires continuous improvement in sports, in school, in our marriages, and in church, but the truth is that pastors and churches notoriously struggle to improve. This struggle to

---

26 David Gavant, *Come Fly With Me* (Jan. 26, 1989), documentary.

improve will ultimately lead to a struggle to grow. Churches struggle to grow because they are more committed to doing things the way they have always been done than they are to improving. This approach has led the church to be in decline. Thousands of churches close their doors every year. The strategies, methods, and approaches that worked ten or twenty years ago are not relevant to people today; however, when you walk into many churches today, it feels like the place is stuck in a past decade—maybe the 70s, 80s, or 90s.

To be clear, I am not talking about adjusting beliefs and teachings to stay relevant to the times. It is a huge mistake to go away from sound biblical teaching to please the changing thought patterns of society. That is the wrong path to church growth. What I am referring to is our methods of doing church. I'm referring to our methods of communication, reaching the community, connecting people to the church, service times, events, how the buildings look, the language we use, the feel, and the smell (yes, smell matters). All these things need improvement—sometimes drastic improvement. But that introduces a problem. As you know, improvement requires change, and change means only one thing. Pain.

Why do pastors struggle to improve things?

As a rule, people don't like change. In a church, if you change the color of the carpet in your auditorium, there is a good chance it could be the topic of next month's elder meeting! That's probably an exaggeration, but maybe not. People don't like change, especially in church. Maybe they feel that the way things are done in church is sacred and, therefore, must stay the same. Maybe they feel emotionally connected to the way things are because that's the way things were when they came to Christ. Maybe they are confused about what is personal preference as opposed to critical to the mission?

As a result, it is hard to make improvements in the church because when we do, there is a backlash. Pastors struggle to make the needed improvements because we fear that backlash. We know it can lead to people leaving, losing resources, and drama—lots of drama. It's safer to keep things the same and avoid the pain.

The result is we don't improve the things that need to be improved and changed. We don't let the staff member go who needs to be let go. We don't restructure the way authority is handled to make better and quicker decisions. We don't improve the way the offering is received. We don't change the way the inside of the building looks. We don't cancel the program that has run its course. We don't start a new ministry that might create a breakthrough. Business as usual continues, and as a result, the church stagnates. Regardless of the difficulties of change, continuous improvement is a must if the church is going to grow. The following are five decisions you need to make to ensure continuous improvement is a regular part of your culture.

DECISION 1: MUSTER THE COURAGE

Back in 2007, about a year after our senior pastor transition, I knew we needed to make some big changes in our music if we were ever going to reach people far from God in the future. Those changes had to begin with the person in charge of the worship department at the time. He was one of the nicest guys in the world. And boy, did he know how to lead a choir! Our choir at the time was between sixty and seventy strong. They practiced every Monday night for two hours.

Our service was televised back then, and it was polished. When I took over, our Worship Pastor had been on staff for seventeen years. He was the same age as my dad. Everyone loved him. There was only one problem—I knew in my heart that to reach new people, we were going to have to move away from that style of music. Not only did we need to move away from that style, but I also knew that he was not the person to take us in the new direction that was needed.

I had to muster the courage as a young, twenty-nine-year-old pastor to walk into this seasoned Worship Pastor's office and have "the" conversation. It was one of the hardest conversations I have ever had to do. Although he was disappointed, he was gracious and, over the next few months, transitioned to another church.

Despite the fact that the decision was necessary, there was a price to it. I knew there would be, but I didn't know how high. Picture an entire choir of sixty to seventy people having their leader asked to move. Yeah, I don't have to say much more, do I? We probably lost an additional two hundred people or more over that one decision. But looking back on it, it was still the right move. We had to make difficult changes in the areas of music and worship to align with our vision to reach people far from God. We could not afford to stay the same. In the short term, we went backward, but I knew we were setting ourselves up for growth in the future.

Continuous improvement requires these types of difficult decisions, and these types of decisions require courage. There is always a risk that the church could go backward for a while, and you could be viewed in a bad light. You must have enough courage to put your "big-boy pants" on and take that risk. It's the only way to move forward.

DECISION 2: STAY CURRENT AND RELEVANT

The choice to stay current and relevant is critical to growing your church. People are looking for something that makes sense in their lives and will make a difference. The gospel must remain the gospel, but it must be explained in a way that makes sense to a changing culture. The apostle Paul explained in 1 Corinthians 9 that whenever he was with Jews, Gentiles, the strong or the weak, he would adjust to their ways without compromising truth to connect them to the gospel. He writes, "Yes, I try to find common ground with everyone, doing everything I can to save some. I do everything to spread the Good News and share in its blessings" (1 Corinthians 9:22-23).

Staying relevant means that people can connect. It means that when people walk into your church, things make sense to them. They make sense not just to believers but to unbelievers as well. It does not mean that they agree with everything, but it means that they understand it and can connect with it. When your church is relevant, people will engage and they will bring their friends.

Staying current and relevant includes things like the interior and exterior of your building, the seating, the stage, the sound, the smell, the function of the building, the music, engaging kids and student ministries, the lighting, the order of service, and the presentation of the message.

That means that all these things must be continuously improving and changing. The question we ask ourselves as a team is, "Does this space, event, illustration, video, song, explanation, or childcare check-in system make sense?" If it only makes sense to insiders or the already-convinced, you have a problem. The people you are trying to reach will not stick around very long if what the church is offering does not connect with their lives.

DOES YOUR CHURCH MAKE SENSE TO UNCHURCHED OR DECHURCHED PEOPLE? IF NOT, IT WILL BE HARD TO GROW YOUR CHURCH.

Pastor, think through the experience your church is offering to people who are unchurched or dechurched. What do they feel when they pull into the parking lot? When they walk into the lobby? When they check in their kids to the kids' ministry? When they enter the bathroom? When they hear the music, or when the message is presented? Those environments and experiences may make sense to you and the people who have been there for a while, but what about a first-time guest? Do those environments and experiences make sense to them? Do they feel comfortable? Does your church make sense to them? If not, it will be hard to grow your church.

DECISION 3: EXCEED EXPECTATIONS

Everyone has expectations when they walk into a church. Thankfully, most people you are trying to reach have low expectations. The people you are trying to reach are probably a lot like the people our church is trying to reach. They are not unchurched but rather dechurched, meaning that they have had a poor experience with church in the past, and they are giving it another try. The question to ask is, "What are their expectations? Why did they leave last time?"

Maybe the message didn't connect with them? Maybe the music was terrible? Maybe no one reached out to follow up with them? Maybe they didn't feel welcome? Maybe it wasn't a friendly experience? Maybe the church didn't offer much for their kids? We don't really know. What we do know is that their expectations are probably low, which means that it won't be very hard to give them a better experience.

Here is a quick list of things you can improve on to not only meet their expectations but far exceed them:

- A warm, friendly greeting at the door
- Clean facilities
- Great programming for their kids
- Engaging worship
- Easy-to-use website
- Free coffee
- Creative use of video
- Useful social media content
- A clear and relatable message for their lives
- Humor and fun

Most people who have written off church but have decided to give it another try think their experience is going to be boring, irrelevant, and judgmental. You have a chance to blow them away! If your church is going to overcome their low expectations, you must continuously work to improve the experience. According to the short list above, how well are you doing in exceeding the expectations?

I wish more pastors thought like restaurant owners, at least in part. When you walk into a restaurant for the first time, you walk in with expectations. You want the place to be clean and smell good. You want the server to provide good service and to be friendly. You want the food to come out in a reasonable time. You want it to taste good and the price to be reasonable. You also want to be able to have a conversation with the people you are with, which means the music cannot be too loud. You also want the bathrooms clean because everyone knows the bathrooms tell the rest of the story.

If the restaurant meets all those expectations or exceeds them, you will be back with friends. Restaurants that do this well over a long period of time thrive. Those that don't close their doors. Obviously, the restaurant illustration breaks down for churches because we do not want people to be lifelong customers. We want them to become part of the team and use their gifting to serve the community and build the church; however, it does work for those we are trying to get through the door and come to Christ.

Do you know the expectations of the people you are trying to reach? Is your church meeting those expectations? What would happen if you exceeded those expectations?

At Emmanuel, we try to intentionally exceed expectations where we can; for example, in the lobby, we offer free coffee with flavored creamers. This might seem like a small thing, but it costs us about $70,000 a year across six physical campuses. When you walk into our bathrooms, you will find wonderful-smelling hand soap with scents that change based on the seasons.

In the parking lot, we provide red wagon rides for the little kids from their cars to the church building. The fun and laughter this provides for our littles are priceless! We also provide a nice gift for a guest who attends or serves for the first time. If someone receives Christ, they receive a box in the mail with a Bible, a coffee mug, and helpful information on next steps to get them started.

Of course, we didn't start this way. There was a long period of time when we didn't have the resources to provide these extra touches. Maybe you are there now as well; however, that doesn't mean you cannot exceed expectations in afford-able ways with warm smiles at the door, handwritten notes, host team members to direct traffic, and extra-clean facilities. Many times, exceeding expectations doesn't cost anything but a little extra effort.

DECISION 4: COMMIT TO LEARNING

Years ago, when I found out that Tiger Woods had a coach, I thought it was extremely odd. How could a coach tell Tiger Woods what to do? Tiger could crush any coach anywhere in a round of golf. It didn't make sense to me.

Come to find out, many of the best athletes, CEOs, and top performers have a coach. Why? Because they know that they have weak spots. They know they have room to grow and that they have not reached their potential yet. They are com-mitted to getting even better. Even the best of the best are still learning and improving.

YOU MUST BE CONTINUALLY LEARNING IF YOU ARE GOING TO CONTINUOUSLY IMPROVE.

You must be continually learning if you are going to continuously improve. The way this looks inside the context of a church is that you are asking the following questions: What is the best way to connect people to small groups? What is the most efficient way to train volunteers? How can we get better at increasing your weekly offering? How can we create a healthier staff culture? How can we find better people to fill open positions? How do we develop our staff? How do we launch a campus? How do we let underperforming staff go more effectively? Even if you do these things well, you can learn to do them even better.

Hiring a coach is one way to commit to learning, but it is far from the only way. Another great way to ensure continuous learning is to attend conferences. Each year our staff attends several different conferences to sharpen our systems and processes. Some of the best decisions we have made as a team have come after attending a conference. A few years ago, our leadership team was down at Church of the Highlands' *Grow Conference*. It was at this conference that we learned about the Dream Team (their volunteer team). We had been struggling as a church to create a culture of volunteerism. What we were doing wasn't working as well as we wanted.

Church of the Highlands taught us a new system of recruiting, training, and developing an effective volunteer team. We came home and as a team went to work adjusting what we needed to adjust with the information we had learned. One of the biggest shifts we made was to restructure our volunteers so that all the people who served—regardless of whether they were serving in the coffee area, greeting, kids' ministry, or any other area—were part of one team. We call this team the "Impact Team," and it has become a significant part of growing our church. The truth is that whatever area you are struggling in, someone has already figured it out. It doesn't matter what it is—fundraising, kids' ministry, student ministry, or volunteerism. You do not have to reinvent the wheel.

Another way we learn is to call a church directly. We regularly call other churches who are ahead of us to learn from them in specific areas. What we have found is that these churches are very willing to take our calls and answer questions. They want you to win as well. We have called churches to learn about increasing generosity, getting people in small groups, multisite ministry, and staffing issues. Again, why reinvent the wheel if someone has already figured it out?

Our staff also learns through books. Every year our department heads are taking their teams through multiple books. They alternate from a book on leadership to a book on spiritual growth. Some of our favorites have been *Extreme Ownership* by Jocko Willink and *Renovation of the Heart* by Dallas Willard. We have gotten tremendous value from *Traction* by Gino Wickman and *The 4 Disciplines of Execution* by Chris McChesney, along with *Soul Keeping* by John Ortberg. I love books because they are a relatively cheap option but provide great value for your team.

The key to learning is humility. John Dixon wrote a little book a few years ago called *Humilitas*. It's a fantastic look at humility and its importance. My favorite line in the book is, "What we don't know far exceeds what we do know."[27] That is so true! Not just with church but in life in general.

If true, humility should be our default setting. We should all be walking around on this planet with a learning posture seeking to understand things in a better way. If we did, we just might improve our lives and our churches.

What gets in the way is our pride. Pride runs deep in all of us. Our pride and our ego will prevent us from learning what we need to know to grow our church; unfortunately, it's often the pastor's ego and pride that prevents the team from learning and improving. It seems that if it is not the pastor's idea, then it's not the right idea.

PASTOR, ARE YOU COMMITTED TO THE BEST IDEAS, NO MATTER WHERE THEY COME FROM? OR DOES IT HAVE TO BE YOUR IDEA?

Pastor, are you committed to the best ideas, no matter where they come from? Or does it have to be your idea? One of the best decisions I have ever made is letting go of my ego. Now, it's not completely gone, but it's sufficiently diminished enough for great ideas to flow from other people, books, and other churches. How is your ego doing?

In his book called *Ego Is the Enemy*, Ryan Holiday argues that ego is the enemy because it stops you from learning

---

27 John Dixon, *Humilitas* (Grand Rapids, MI: Zondervan, 2019) 59.

what you need to know.[28] If you already know everything, you cannot learn.

DECISION 5: VALUE THE VISION OVER PREFERENCES

I once heard a pastor say, "When outsiders enter our church, the only thing we want them to stumble over is the cross." I like that statement. I don't totally agree, but I understand the sentiment. He's saying let's be willing to let go of any preference that is not critical to the mission of seeing people get to the cross. The cross is offensive enough.

What does this look like practically? It looks like we ought to be willing to change our music style for the sake of the mission. Worship becomes more of a preference for the already convinced. One Christian may like this style, while another likes that style. What about the style of the unbeliever? That is who you are trying to reach after all.

To be clear, I am not talking about lyrics. All lyrics to worship music should be biblical and true. I'm talking about the style and sound. Music is a powerful tool to connect with people who are far from God. It is very possible to select music that is honoring to God, consistent with Scripture, and relevant to outsiders. When you choose this type of music, you are choosing vision over preference. This requires continuous improvement because music styles are always changing.

Valuing vision over preference also looks like you should be willing to change the way you preach. People who have been Christians for a long time and perhaps grew up in church have become accustomed to hearing a preacher preach in a certain

---

28   Ryan Holiday, *Ego Is the Enemy* (New York, NY: Portfolio, 2016).

way. Maybe a person is used to the pastor preaching through the Bible verse by verse. Maybe the preacher speaks with some fire and brimstone. There is nothing particularly wrong with these methods of preaching other than the fact that they seem to be preferences of the already-convinced or those who have been "insiders" for a very long time.

It has been my experience that many Christians prefer this kind of preaching over a more relatable style, such as topical preaching. They will even leave church over this issue. There is nowhere in the Bible that says the pastor must preach verse by verse. It is not a sin to preach topically; in fact, Jesus taught topically. When preferences become more important than vision, the church will struggle to reach people. Those on the inside will insist that those coming from the outside must like things the way they like them, or else they will have to leave.

Valuing vision over preference also looks like letting go of any programs that are no longer producing results. This is a tough one, because as you already know, church people love their "thing." Their "thing" could be any number of things such as Trunk and Treat, Upward Basketball, Sunday School, the KJV Bible translation, Wednesday night Bible Study, Awana, potluck Sunday lunch, and on and on.

The problem with letting some of these things go is that at one time in the past, these things worked. They were a draw for new people. The church grew as a result, but time has passed, and now these programs and methods are tired, dying, or even dead already.

The problem is that people cannot let them go. Then, you can't let them go because your people can't let them go. But you must let them go because they no longer are working. Yes, it will be painful, but if you consistently reinforce the vision and the "why," over time, people will begin to understand, and it will sink in.

Moses never gave instructions to do Sunday School or Upward Basketball. These are methods that were once successful in bringing new people into your church; however, over time, they have lost their effectiveness. You will lose some families over these changes, and it will be painful. But the vision is worth it.

I remember about eighteen months into our transition. We made the bold decision to move away from using the KJV translation of the Bible. This was a huge change because it was written in our church by-laws that we would only use that version. The elders met for months studying and discussing it. We had to put together a position paper to provide an explanation to the congregation and then bring it before the entire church for a vote. I was terrified. It was part of our culture.

The only problem was that the KJV language did not make sense to outsiders, the very people we were trying to reach. It was risky. The vote went through, and we changed our by-laws, but it did not come without pain. We lost several good families over that decision; however, we were able to make our messages much more understandable to our guests who were unchurched or dechurched, and the church began to grow. You know that your church is beginning to value vision over preference when you can let go of things that have run their course.

Another big improvement we made was with our method of giving. Today, most of our giving is done online through a company called PushPay. A few people still put envelopes in a box at the back of the auditorium, but we no longer pass offering buckets. This was a struggle for years. We feared that if we didn't pass offering buckets, we would lose income. We had also received feedback from members of the church that physical giving was part of their worship experience.

YOU KNOW THAT YOUR CHURCH IS BEGINNING TO VALUE VISION OVER PREFERENCE WHEN YOU CAN LET GO OF THINGS THAT HAVE RUN THEIR COURSE.

Even though there was evidence from other churches that giving online was working and creating even more consistency in giving, we hesitated. The reason was fear. We had to dig deep and embrace the fact that passing the offering bucket was something that created discomfort for our guests. Our commitment was to remove all stumbling blocks except for the truth of God's Word. We made the leap and disappointed some people, but it worked! Since going completely online with our giving, we have not only seen an increase in giving but also a greater level of consistency in giving.

Continuous improvement requires courage because there is a price, especially if your church hasn't developed a taste for change. I joke with pastors sometimes who are just starting to make changes to improve their experience by asking them, "Are you willing to work part-time at Starbucks because that may be what it comes to?"

Change is difficult in the church world. But it is necessary to improve and reach people. Let me encourage you; after you have successfully improved things in the church, and your church reaps the reward with growth, people will begin to reward you with trust. This trust is critical for the next improvement. Once you announce the next thing you are going to improve, they will remember what happened last time and will not push back as hard.

When it comes to improvement, take the long view. People will understand that they are on a winning team, and winning requires improvement. They will stop assuming that you are changing things for the sake of change. They will trust you. If you keep pointing them back to the vision as the reason for the change, they will understand. Over time they will become just as zealous as you are to remove any obstacles standing in the way of their friends and family coming to Christ.

Chapter 7

YOUR HEALTH

*"Take care of your body. It's the only place
you have to live."*

—Jim Rohn

I want to talk to you about your health—specifically, taking care
of your body. It may seem odd to see this in a book about church
growth, but there is a significant connection between how a pastor
takes care of his body and the growth of his church.

In this chapter, I will unpack that connection. Let's start with
reality. The Barna Research Group has reported that 50% of
pastors are unhealthy, overweight, and do not exercise.[29] Another
study found this: "Food addiction and obesity is the #1 problem
with ministers."[30] As a whole, pastors do a poor job stewarding
their bodies. This really doesn't make a whole lot of sense when
we consider that Paul explained that "Your body is the temple of
the Holy Spirit, who lives in you," and therefore, you "must honor
God with your body" (1 Corinthians 6:19-20).

---

29 "Statistics for Pastors," *Pastoral Care Inc.*, www.pastoralcareinc.com/statistics/.
30 "Pastoral Addictions," *Resources and Support for Ministers and Pastors*, www.pastoralcareinc.com/
pastoral-addictions/.

Let me ask you a question. Can a pastor successfully lead a team of people to grow a church, handle all the problems and stress, and lead a church to reach its full potential while not feeling well most of the time? While having low energy? While feeling discouraged by the way he or she looks? I believe the answer is no.

The reality is that when pastors are unhealthy in their bodies, it's a good indication that they are unhealthy in other areas. Staying healthy takes discipline, but so does managing a budget, creating a healthy staff culture, keeping a marriage on track, raising children, and staying sexually pure. According to Pastoral Care, Inc., "4 in 10 pastors view pornography daily."[31] This is a terrible statistic, but it does not shock me because a lack of discipline in one area usually manifests itself in other areas.

According to Lifeway Research:

- Almost 3,000 pastors leave the ministry each year; and
- 250 pastors leave the ministry each month.[32]

To be clear, there are many reasons why pastors quit. Some of them include discouragement, financial stress, political tension in the church, loneliness, moral failures, burnout, and poor physical health. The challenges of pastors today require a pastor to be healthy spiritually, emotionally, and physically, and to be able to switch quickly between difficult tasks.

Scott McConnell, from Lifeway Research, explains that, "The demand on a pastor requires them to quickly switch between different complex tasks that require completely different knowledge, skills, and abilities."

---

31 "Pastoral Addictions," *Resources and Support for Ministers and Pastors.*
32 Mark Dance, "Pastors Are Not Quitting in Droves," 10 Jul 2019, *Lifeway Research,* https://research.lifeway.com/2019/07/10/pastors-are-not-quitting-in-droves-2/.

McConnell quotes Matt Bloom, an Associate Professor at the University of Notre Dame, saying that the "switching is costly in terms of cognitive effort, behavior control, and emotional regulation." A normal day for a pastor often includes preparing a message, speaking with a congregant about the loss of a loved one, a lunch meeting to raise funds, responding to a negative email, and a difficult conversation with a staff member.

McConnell then says, "The list of tasks for a pastor never ends. There is always another complex task to switch to and to pour your all into."[33] Is it any wonder why 38% of pastors are thinking about quitting? Or that only 1 out of every 10 pastors will retire as a pastor?

9Marks cited this finding from Schaeffer Institute: "50% of pastors feel so discouraged that they would leave the ministry if they could, but have no other way of making a living."[34]

What if it were true that the reason many pastors struggle is because they don't feel well or lack the energy necessary to meet the never-ending list of demands? Sometimes I wonder if poor physical health is not only one of the reasons pastors quit, but perhaps also the catalyst for some of the other reasons. If this is true, is it possible to mitigate some of our struggles by simply maintaining a healthy body?

Certainly, we must take care of our souls, and we covered that in Chapter 1. But what about our bodies? Isn't our body the home of our soul? Indeed, it is. I do not believe that the soul and the body are the same thing. The soul departs from the body at

---

33 Scott McConnell, "Are More Pastors Quitting Today?", *Lifeway research*, 13 May 2021, https://research.lifeway.com/2021/05/13/are-more-pastors-quitting-today/.

34 Thabiti Anyabwile, "Don't Make Your Pastor a Statistic," *9Marks*, 10 June 2014, https://www.9marks.org/article/dont-make-your-pastor-a-statistic/.

death; however, the soul and body are so closely intertwined that they work together.

SOMETIMES I WONDER IF POOR PHYSICAL HEALTH IS NOT ONLY ONE OF THE REASONS PASTORS QUIT, BUT PERHAPS ALSO THE CATALYST FOR SOME OF THE OTHER REASONS.

Have you ever felt so scared that your body shook in fear? Our thoughts, feelings, and bodies are linked together. In a very real sense, your body is either working for you or against you, hindering you or helping you. This is the danger of addiction. Addiction doesn't start as addiction; it starts with a behavior. When that behavior is repeated, the body begins to have a mind of its own. It starts to crave whatever you have been feeding it. What started as a choice in your mind has now become an appetite in the body. This is the body working against you and not for you.

Years ago, I had my right knee ACL repaired. I had torn it completely while playing in a basketball game. When the injury happened, it was one of the most painful things I ever experienced. It felt like a hot knife that stabbed into the center of my knee from the side. After the surgery came the recovery. It was brutal. The pain seemed like it would never go away.

My poor wife took care of me while I lay on the couch day after day, week after week. Interestingly, I thought I would be able to get back to work in about a week. I mean, it was just one small tendon in my knee. What I hadn't anticipated was the reality of how bad I would feel emotionally. I couldn't think. Food didn't taste good. The pain stopped me from being able to concentrate. My immobility began affecting my mood. My normal joyful perspective was slowly fading into a consistent discouragement. The bottom line was that my physical health was hindering my spiritual health. The pain was blocking me from any pastoral work. I added little to no value to the church for six weeks! The physical affects the mental and emotional.

When we feel bad, our performance suffers. My knee surgery is an extreme example, but it makes my point. For some reason this makes sense for professional athletes, but not pastors. An athlete's number one job is to take care of his or her body for obvious reasons. They need their bodies to work for maximum productivity. But isn't this true for everyone else including pastors? Indeed, it is! So why do we eat terrible foods, skip exercise, and neglect sleep? Why do we think we can neglect our bodies and still perform at high levels?

WHY DO WE THINK WE CAN NEGLECT OUR BODIES AND STILL PERFORM AT HIGH LEVELS?

If you want to grow your church, there are four reasons you should value your physical health.

1. A HEALTHY BODY GIVES YOU ENERGY

When you take care of your body, it responds by giving you energy, and energy is what you need to meet the demands of a growing church. According to *Facts and Factors*, in 2021, the global energy drink market was 46 billion dollars.[35] It is projected to be 108 billion by 2028. This is a staggering number, and I believe it reveals just how unhealthy and energy-deficient people are. We need energy and lots of it to write sermons, help people in need, and creatively solve problems. God has wired you to have sufficient energy to do what you need through four key activities—maintaining a nutritious diet, staying hydrated, exercising, and sleeping.

Years ago, I attended a pastoral retreat that was focused on three key areas—leadership, emotional health, and physical fitness. The retreat brought in an expert who had a PhD in health and its connection to work. His name was Jack Groppel. I was absolutely fascinated with how he connected our physical health with our ability to lead.

I walked away with the conviction that being in top physical shape could improve my leadership by up to 30%. He made it clear that leaders who are in top physical shape made better decisions, had more stamina, and handled stress much better than leaders who were out of shape. The truth is we were not designed to get by on caffeine. Mountains of research have been piled up to show that exercise, hydration, proper diet, and rest produce the energy you need to function at your best.

---

35 "Energy Drinks Market Size, Growth, Global Trends, Forecast to 2028," *Facts and Factors*, Sept. 2022, www.fnfresearch.com/energy-drinks-market.

Pastor, how are your energy levels these days? On a scale of 1-10, where is your energy? How much of that 7 is supported by stimulants like caffeine? If your answer was 7 or below, I can tell you that there are some adjustments that need to be made. Your church is losing because you are not at full strength. Are you getting enough sleep? Are you drinking enough water? How is your vegetable intake? How about your workout routine? If you are missing the mark, don't be discouraged. No one is batting a thousand in this area. You can make some simple adjustments that will get quick results. I am going to walk through those in the next few pages. You can and must change.

2. A HEALTHY BODY SERVES AS A GREAT EXAMPLE TO YOUR CONGREGATION

You are the leader, and you carry the most influence. This is how God has ordered things. I believe that many Christians neglect their bodies today, and they lack the ability to see how they treat their bodies as a spiritual issue because their pastor hasn't led by example. It pains me to say this, but my greatest influence in our church is not my preaching. It's how I live. The same is true for you.

It's our overall lifestyle that makes the biggest difference with our people. If they see us poking fun at people who exercise and then carry an additional fifty to one hundred pounds around on our own bodies, we are essentially giving them the green light to do the same.

Your congregation needs to not only hear you teach that they need to honor God with their bodies, but they also need to see what that looks like from you. You might be thinking, *How does maintaining a healthy body grow the church?* Great question! This is how it has worked for us.

I have been going to the same gym for over ten years. It's about four miles from our broadcast campus. Over this time, I have been able to develop many relationships with people and invite them to the church. The gym has almost become a campus for us because I feel like I do more actual ministry there than I do in the church building. I don't know how many people from the gym have come to church over the years because of a simple invitation, but there are many.

The sauna is my favorite place to do ministry because you have a captive audience. You are in a small room with a few other guys, almost naked. It's intimate, very intimate. Lots of questions are asked. Guys open up. It seems like almost every week I have a new story about someone who has been moved toward Christ because of a conversation in the sauna.

Just this past week, one of our campus pastors shared a story about a man who was going to be baptized because I invited him to church in the sauna! My stories from the sauna have become legendary, and our congregation looks forward to them, which I think is hilarious. They've even been coined, "Stories from the sauna." How did this happen? It was because of a simple decision to value my physical fitness.

FOOD, EXERCISE, AND REST ARE SPIRITUAL ISSUES. WHEN WE NEGLECT OUR HEALTH, WE ARE DISHONORING THE BODY GOD GAVE US.

Valuing health and fitness also grows the individuals who already attend your church. Self-control or discipline is required to maintain a healthy body, and it is, after all, a fruit of the Spirit. We must teach our congregations that how we treat our bodies is part of our discipleship. Food, exercise, and rest are spiritual issues. When we neglect our health, we are dishonoring the body God gave us. Have you taught on these issues lately? Do you model good physical fitness and a healthy lifestyle? If not, it's time to make some changes.

3. A HEALTHY BODY GIVES YOU CONFIDENCE

A strong, healthy leader is humble and gracious. He is also confident. Not boastful or egotistical, just quietly confident in what he is doing and Whom he is doing it for. The reality of the human situation is that the way we look impacts how we function. This is why we spend time on our appearance. Before we go out, we make sure we like our clothes, shoes, and hair. It matters to us, and that does not make us shallow or narcissistic. We want to look our best because when we look our best, we feel more confident around those we lead and serve.

Not long ago I was observing a pastor giving a sermon. He was doing very well, but about every other sentence, he was pulling on his shirt. It was a distraction to his audience. His concern was that his shirt was going to get caught in some of his . . . let's say, extra skin. Is that kind enough? Anyone watching could tell what his concern was. His audience was distracted because he was unsure and a little embarrassed about his appearance.

You may think this is being shallow, but I assure you it is not. We are human beings who care about the way we look. The way you look matters. Your confidence matters. When you have done the work to be in good shape, you will feel better about yourself, and you will, by default, do better work.

When you lack confidence, you can become like that very insecure person you know. You know the one I'm talking about—that person who is shy, sort of backward, and low-risk. Or, like that other insecure person you know who is defensive, overly critical, and always putting others down to make themselves feel better. Either way, low-confidence people make difficult friends and even worse leaders. You don't want to be either. Build healthy confidence by taking care of your body.

4. A HEALTHY BODY GIVES YOU LONGEVITY

Growing your church takes time, lots of time. At the writing of this book, I am in my eighteenth year of leading our church. It has taken almost two decades to grow from nine hundred to just under seven thousand in weekly attendance. I know there are stories out there of churches exploding in five years. I believe those are the outliers. The typical story of a church that has grown in tremendous ways is a long story covering between twenty and thirty years.

Consider this next number: the average pastor lasts four years in his position before moving on or quitting. As I mentioned earlier, there are lots of reasons pastors leave the ministry or move on, such as loneliness, anger, moral failures, and betrayals to name a few. In eighteen years, I have faced all of these at some level. I believe that taking care of my soul has played a huge part in staying in the game. I also believe that being healthy has played just as big of a role.

WHEN YOU EAT RIGHT, EXERCISE, AND SLEEP WELL, YOUR CAPACITY TO HANDLE STRESS AND PROBLEMS INCREASES.

When you eat right, exercise, and sleep well, your capacity to handle stress and problems increases. You not only have the physical energy you need, but you also build your emotional energy. The body and the soul work together. When I am stressed out and feeling overwhelmed, a good workout coupled with a good night's sleep give me the recovery and energy I need to face the issues the next day. Growing your church is a long game. If you want to be around in ten years, functioning at your full capacity, you must take care of your body.

Make it a priority and drop the excuses.

Taking care of your health comes down to making it your priority. That is where a big part of the problem lies. Pastors have a never-ending list of things to do. First, the pastors have the normal weekly task of preparing the message, meeting with teams, responding to emails, and pushing projects forward. Then there are the unexpected things that happen—the deaths and marriage crises that must be responded to. At any given time, there may be three or four or five of these fires burning, each one demanding your attention. It is so easy to simply rationalize that you don't have time for a workout. You don't have time to think through a healthy meal plan. So, what do we do? We skip the workout, and we eat on the run, often fast food. Any pastor can fall into this trap of making excuses for why they are not taking care of their bodies.

The truth of the matter is that we haven't made being healthy a priority. We have not decided that our health is a key contributor to successful leadership, and because we haven't made that decision, other things take up our time. If you want to be healthy, you must make health your priority. Making health your priority looks like this:

First, it looks like scheduling a daily workout. Your workout goes on the schedule before anything else, much like your devotional time in the morning. It is non-negotiable. My workout is every day at 4:30 or 5:00 p.m. Unless someone has died, I head to the gym at that time.

Second, it looks like you eat for fuel, not pleasure (80% of the time). This requires homework and preparation. You must study and discover what food gives you the greatest return on nutrients. Purchase those foods and make a meal plan. Try to plan out what you will be eating at least twenty-four hours in advance. Prepping meals for the week is the best way to go, but this takes extreme planning and discipline.

What you are trying to avoid is leaving your eating choices up to the moment when you are hungry. This leaves you to pick the most pleasurable food which will most likely be pizza or a burger with fries.

Third, it looks like drinking a gallon of water a day. Many experts say ninety ounces is enough, but I like to go past that amount to ensure that I am thoroughly hydrated at all times. Every organ in your body, especially your brain, is mostly water. Each organ needs plenty of water to function properly and at full capacity. I always carry a liter water bottle with me and refill it once it's empty.

Lastly, prioritizing your health looks like going to bed early. Since we must get up early, going to bed early looks like 10:30 p.m. for most. If you sleep for seven hours, which is recommended by many experts, you will be able to start your day at 5:30 am. You may not need seven hours of sleep, but I assure you that you are not superhuman, gifted with the ability to function on five hours or less. Eventually, your body will pay you back for not giving it the rest it needs. There are times when we must forgo sleep to serve well, but those times must be the exception, not the rule.

IT HAS BEEN SAID, "WE FIRST MAKE OUR HABITS, AND THEN OUR HABITS MAKE US." IF YOU WANT TO BE HEALTHY, YOU MUST MAKE IT YOUR PRIORITY.

You are not going to do this perfectly every day. No one does; however, as you practice these disciplines, they will begin to become habits for you. And that is where the magic happens. The struggle ends when you begin to take care of your body without even thinking about it. That is, after all, what a habit is. It has been said, "We first make our habits, and then our habits make us." If you want to be healthy, you must make it your priority.

When it comes to exercise, find something you love.

So many people don't exercise because they hate the treadmill, can't stand to run, despise the Stairmaster, and find the elliptical boring. I have done all these exercises, and I can empathize. None of them are exhilarating. Most of them are boring unless you have a great podcast to listen to, which I highly recommend. If you find yourself in this situation, the solution is simple. Don't do those things. Do something else. Find a workout partner and lift weights. Get a few friends together and play basketball. Start going to cycling classes with a group. Join a gym that has a pool and start swimming for thirty minutes a day. There are so many options. Even walking for between thirty-five and forty minutes a day is better than nothing.

For the first four years of my ministry career as a youth pastor, I had small kids and was crazy busy. I was young and figured that I didn't have to work out. I consumed extraordinary amounts of pizza, chips, and soda. I hardly drank any water. Over time I began to see my body change, and I noticed that I was tired all the time.

I decided to make a change. That's when I discovered running. At first, I was terrible, but slowly, I got in better and better shape. It wasn't long before I ran my first half-marathon. I fell in love with running. I started a subscription to *Runner's World*, bought books, and began reading about a diet that would help me run faster and with more stamina. I was hooked. From the age of twenty-six until I was thirty-six, I ran ten half-marathons and one full marathon. Running became my passion, and, as a result, I was in the best shape of my life.

Well, as we know, all good things must come to an end, especially as you age. All the running took its toll on my knees, and running became too painful. So, around the age of thirty-five, I started lifting weights. The same scenario unfolded as with running. At first, I was weak, skinny, and felt out of place. But as I gave it time and did some research, I began to enjoy it. I started to build some muscle and felt like I fit in. Today, I am still lifting weights almost daily and loving it. I mix in some cardio by playing some pick-up basketball a few times a week which is another passion of mine.

Why do I share this? To me, it's not really exercise. It's fun. I love doing it, so it does not seem like a burden or another thing I must squeeze into my day. It's quite the opposite. I look forward to my daily workout because I know I'm going to have fun while I'm there, and it's going to make me feel good. You can do the same thing. Experiment with different things until you find an activity that you really love. Remember to give it time because you might be terrible and feel out of place at first.

Find a few healthy people and hang out with them.

One of my favorite quotes is from Jim Rohn. He said, "You're the average of the five people you spend the most time with."[36] Today I am the average of my five closest friends and so are you. Think about it. You are probably within ten to fifteen pounds of what they weigh. You probably make within ten to fifteen thousand dollars of what they make. You probably live in a similar neighborhood with a similar car. You are probably close in age and have kids that are close in age.

Of course, there are exceptions. Several of my really good friends are grandpas. That is a long way off for me, but for the

---

36 Aimee Groth, "You're the Average of the Five People You Spend the Most Time With," *Business Insider*, 24 July 2012, www.businessinsider.com/jim-rohn-youre-the-average-of-the-five-people-you-spend-the-most-time-with-2012-7.

most part, this is true. People become like their friends. We preach this to our people because it's true.

If you want to be healthy, you must get around healthy people. Two of my closest friends are health nuts. They hit the gym daily and text pictures of their meals to each other. I must admit, I am part of the group chat, full disclosure. It's a little over the top, but it keeps me on track, eating the right foods and getting my workouts in. I don't want to fall behind these guys, and in a very real sense, I feed off their affirmation and encouragement. To say it bluntly, they fire me up with their commitment to feeling and looking their best. These guys have taught me what proper nutrition looks like and how to efficiently and effectively work out for maximum results.

At the end of the day, pastors are notorious for poor health. According to Dr. Richard J. Krejcir of the Shaeffer Institute, only one in ten pastors will retire as pastors.[37] Is there a connection between the two? I believe there is. When you are taking care of your body, you feel better, have more energy, think more clearly, feel more confident, and are much more equipped to handle stress. Your body is the house of your soul. They work together.

YOUR BODY IS THE HOUSE OF YOUR SOUL. THEY WORK TOGETHER.

We must work to take care of both our souls and our bodies if we want to function at full capacity. When you take care of your

---

37 Dr. Richard J. Krejcir cited in "Don't Make Your Pastor a Statistic."

body, you are honoring God and providing a good example for your congregation to follow. Leading your church to reach its full potential and reaching people with the gospel is a long game. It takes decades. Your body must be able to hold up over the long haul. That part is up to you. Taking care of your health is the first step in leadership. It's self-leadership, and it's time to get it done.

Chapter 8

THE POWER OF A HOBBY

If you have read this far, you know by now that growing your church will require everything you have. You will have to pour your heart, soul, mind, and strength into the endeavor. The challenge will demand that you carefully care for both your soul and body. Significant growth in your church will include years and even decades filled with highs and lows; however, as you have already decided, it's all worth it to see people come to Christ and grow in Christ. Nothing in all the world is more important than working with God to advance His rule and reign on this earth.

THE WORK WE DO CAN CONSUME US IF WE ARE NOT CAREFUL.

The work we do can consume us, however, if we are not careful. The ministry, with all its twists and turns, ups and downs, can eat you alive. Your church can become all you think about all the time. Your mind can become consumed with your next sermon, the latest tragedy, a conflict on your staff, the next event, and the money that needs to be raised for the latest building project.

The issues and challenges never end; in fact, as your church grows, you will only face more difficulties and challenges, and these difficulties and challenges only get more complicated. That's why every ministry leader must learn how to handle the stress that comes along with the growing challenges. Taking care of your soul and body are critical ways to handle that stress. In this chapter, I want to discuss a less-often talked about solution to managing the stresses that come along with growth. I'm talking about the power of taking up a hobby.

According to *Webster's Dictionary*, a hobby is "a pursuit outside one's regular occupation engaged in especially for relaxation."[38] I love this definition because it not only describes what a hobby is, but it also tells us *why* we should do it. I talk to so many pastors who do not know how to relax and truly disconnect from ministry. They cannot "turn it off" by their own admission. The truth is that we can become so accustomed to always being engaged with whatever needs to be handled that we literally do not know how to stop ourselves from working. Based on my own experience as a pastor and working with other pastors in a coaching relationship for the past eight years, I could make a strong argument that many pastors are workaholics.

I believe the reason we find it almost impossible to turn things off is because there really is no end to the work. Sunday is always just seven days away, and there are always three to five unresolved

---

38 "Hobby," *Merriam-Webster*, https://www.merriam-webster.com/dictionary/hobby.

issues at hand. Over time, many pastors give in to the expectation that they are "always available" to the people they serve.

The mindset that we are "always available" to those we serve means we will fail to create boundaries and finish lines. We will become afraid to disappoint people, and our phones will never stop buzzing. Thus, our "on switch" will always be on.

I believe hobbies are one of God's time-tested ways of helping us to disconnect from working and avoid becoming workaholics. You may be reading this right now thinking to yourself, *I'm not even sure what it would feel like to relax and disconnect.* If that's you, your problem is that your "on switch" has been on so long that you have forgotten what it's like to just be a normal person who can enjoy activities outside of pastoral work.

That is not a good place to be. If you don't learn how to turn things off and relax your mind and body on a regular basis, it won't be long before you burn out and leave the ministry. You might last a few years because you're gritty, young, and you love energy drinks, but eventually, the wear and tear and the emotional weight will be just too heavy for anything other than a healthy and rested soul.

Do You Think You Are Too Busy?

Many pastors will say that they are too busy to have a hobby. I find this response a little bit humorous and very troubling because it reveals just how deep the problem goes. We have become so addicted to activity that we have convinced ourselves that we are always needed at the church. We think, *If I leave for one or two hours, the place might collapse.* Seriously?

THE "I'M TOO BUSY" EXCUSE IS ONE OF TWO THINGS: IT'S EITHER AN OVERVALUING OF ONE'S IMPORTANCE OR A FAILURE IN LEADERSHIP TO DEVELOP A TEAM AND EMPOWER OTHERS.

The "I'm too busy" excuse is one of two things: it's either an overvaluing of one's importance or a failure in leadership to develop a team and empower others. Pastor, either way, it's an excuse that is not valid. If the President of the United States can find time to have a hobby, so can you.

HOW DO HOBBIES HELP US RELAX?

How exactly do hobbies help us to relax and disconnect? In *The Power of Hobbies*, Steph Miller, a systemic kinesiologist, explains what happens when you are engaging in a hobby:

> *You are living in the moment. As a result, you are not dwelling on your past or worrying about your future. This is psychologically one of the best places to be. . . . We are more likely to be able to switch off and relax during stressful times.*[39]

I could not agree more. A hobby is the "switch off" button. It is the way you call a "timeout" in ministry and regather.

If you have played sports when you were younger, you know how important a timeout can be. In baseball, when a pitcher is giving up hit after hit, the coach will call timeout and go out to

---

[39] Steph Miller, "The Power of Hobbies," *Medium*, 16 June 2017, medium.com/thrive-global/the-power-of-hobbies-steph-miller-92f5811b1a5f.

the mound and have a talk. His goal is to check on his pitcher to see if he is okay. Is he frazzled? Is he hurt? Can he continue? Does he just need a moment to clear his head? This walk to the mound gives the coach the perspective he needs to either keep his guy in the game or signal for relief. Timeouts give you space—the space to breathe, gain perspective, and recover. This is the power of a hobby.

Let me ask you a question. What is your hobby? What activity do you engage in that helps you to "switch off" the ministry button for a while? If you don't have one, you need one. One of the reasons you may not have one is simply that no one has ever given you permission to have one.

Well, I will be that person for you. A hobby is so important that I would say that it is just as important to your longevity in ministry as a consistent quiet time and good friends. At this point in my ministry career, twenty-three years in, I would attribute my vitality and longevity to three things: my spiritual practices, my relationships, and my hobbies.

THE POWER OF HOBBIES

Being in ministry can feel like you are on a treadmill that just doesn't stop. The truth is that no one is going to slow it down or turn it off for you to get a break; in fact, the opposite is quite true. As people gain more and more access to you, they will turn up the speed and fully expect you to keep up. God has given us the dynamic of hobbies to be able to mentally detach from the work of ministry and slow down.

The truth is that your mind needs a break. No one can stay on the treadmill every day, all day, even if it's just in your mind. You may practice Sabbath one day a week, but even then, many times you are thinking about church work and people who need help. How do I know? Because I have done that for years. I'm off, but not really off. This is where hobbies are extremely helpful.

When you are engaged in a hobby you love, like running, writing, or rock climbing, your attention is completely taken off the challenges and difficulties of the day and week. A good hobby allows you to fully engage your heart and mind in a different direction away from people needing your help, prayer, or support. When done correctly, you can forget about the weight and stress of church work for a while.

This little break that lasts for thirty minutes up to two hours or so will allow your mind and emotions to experience the break they need to recover. Almost like magic, you can come back to the business of growing your church with a new freshness and vitality. Often, I will return to a problem that I have been stuck on with a solution I hadn't been able to think of before.

In order for a hobby to have this effect, it must include an element of fun or at least enjoyment. One of my hobbies is playing basketball. I am now forty-six and not nearly as fast or athletic as I once was. But I can still compete with most of the guys at the gym I frequent. Yes, I'm sore the next day after playing 3-on-3, but I don't care. Why? Because it is a blast. I love to compete and try to win. I love to try to develop my shot. I love to try to improve my accuracy. It feels great. It's healthy to run, and I play with people I enjoy. And having a plate full of pancakes after basketball on Fridays makes it even better. No one is trying to go to the NBA, so we do not play hard defense. It's all in good fun. Basketball, for me, is an escape. It allows me to feel like I'm a "normal" person who is just like everyone else, at least for a little while.

If you struggle to find a hobby, just look back into your past and ask yourself what you once loved to do. Did you once love to hike? Paint? Read? Write? (I wish I enjoyed writing. This book would have been written ten years ago). Cycling? Hunting? Fishing? There are endless options. You just must find one you love and start practicing it.

A HOBBY GIVES YOU A SENSE OF CONTROL

As pastors, we talk a lot about surrendering control of our lives to God. We challenge our people to surrender, and we try to model a surrendered life. This, of course, is right and true; however, there is a real need for leaders to have some sense of control and completion over events in their lives and churches.

What am I talking about? Isn't that God's role? Yes, it is; however, there is something essential to the life of any leader, and that is to see some kind of finished result for the work that they have put in. Everyone wants to see a reward for their labor. This is why it feels so good to look over a freshly cut lawn after two hours of mowing.

Seeing your labor get results and the sense of satisfaction that comes from your labor is vital to our emotional and psychological health. This dynamic is hard to come by in ministry work. All too often pastors feel like they are ER doctors responding to the latest crisis.

It is our responsibility to grow the church. We are in charge of leading the team, casting vision, and developing the strategy to execute and fulfill the vision. We are responsible for getting results. That is the job of the leader, but as you know, if you have led for any length of time, it is extremely hard to see how any of the things you are doing are actually moving the needle.

The reality is that most of what we do has a delayed effect on growth. We make a decision or make a hire, and the results lag. We start a campaign to raise money for a project, and we don't see a change for months. We preach a series on spiritual growth, but it's hard to measure if it worked. Ministry is a job that often seems disconnected from outcomes and because of this, many pastors can feel like what they are doing is not making a difference. The feeling of accomplishment and completion is rare; therefore, feelings of satisfaction and fulfillment can be sparse.

This is where a hobby helps. A healthy hobby provides that emotional health. Let's say, for example, your hobby is repairing old cars or carving wood. You put in two good hours of work on the car, and after it's over, you can step back and actually see what you did. The work that you put in produced a specific result—and that result brings you pleasure.

YOUR TIME SPENT ENGAGING IN A HOBBY CREATES A CHANGE, AND GOD HAS WIRED US IN SUCH A WAY THAT WE FIND SATISFACTION IN THAT CHANGE.

Your time spent engaging in a hobby creates a change, and God has wired us in such a way that we find satisfaction in that change. One of my favorite hobbies today is lifting weights. By no means am I a muscle head. I don't have the body for it. I am 6 foot 3 inches tall with a thin frame. No strongest-man competitions are in my future; however, I really enjoy learning about how to make my body stronger and build muscle. I enjoy the work that is required to build my body. I find it very satisfying to know that if I do certain workouts and eat a certain diet, I can see a difference in my body. The work I am doing is getting results.

How does this help? Well, no matter what craziness is going on at church, no matter how out of control things may seem to be, I can always retreat to the gym and control something. For about an hour a day, my entire focus comes off the problems of ministry, and I get to work on something else. It really helps that I find lifting weights fun as well.

A HOBBY IS A GREAT WAY TO DEVELOP FRIENDSHIPS

In the next chapter, I am going to dive into the need to have friends. For now, I just want to point out that a hobby doesn't have to be something you do alone. It is a great way to develop and deepen a friendship. My two favorite hobbies are basketball and weightlifting. I often engage in these hobbies by myself; however, I also include other people who I enjoy being with. Playing basketball and lifting weights with my friends provides the added benefits of fun, competition, and laughter—lots of laughter. And we all need to laugh more. I know it's hard to find friends with whom you can just be yourself; in fact, it may seem impossible. I assure you it's not. Just don't give up. Keep working at it until you find a few people who will allow you to "let your hair down." Basketball is fun by myself, but it's a blast with my friends!

A HOBBY MAKES YOU FEEL NORMAL

As I mentioned above, a hobby can help you to feel like a normal person. Do you remember when you were a kid, and you saw one of your teachers in the grocery store? Do you remember thinking, *What is she doing here?* Your teacher wasn't a normal person. She was not supposed to be in the grocery store. She should be in the classroom, right? That sort of thing happens to those of us in ministry. People often do not think of us as normal people who drive cars, go to movies, and eat food. We are to be at the church praying and reading the Bible and preaching sermons.

The reactions and responses people have when they see us in public reinforce this dynamic. A real danger is that we can begin to conform to this perception. We can even start to feel weird about being in public. A hobby has a way of breaking down that perception, especially when you talk about your hobbies in your sermons. A hobby reminds you and allows you to be you. You are not a ministry machine that preaches and does weddings, funerals, counseling, and Bible studies all day, every day. You are a normal person with a variety of interests and passions.

MAKE TIME FOR YOUR HOBBY

All too often pastors and ministry leaders see a hobby as something that they will get to if they have time. This is ridiculous because you will never have time. You must make time. There is always, and I repeat always, something important that you should be doing. Someone who needs your help. An email that needs to be responded to. A note that needs to be written. An issue regarding your staff that needs your attention.

YOUR HOBBY IS A FORM OF SELF-CARE.

Considering this reality, you must put it on your schedule as an appointment. Mark it down like you would any other meeting. Why? Because your hobby is a form of self-care. It allows you to break away from stress and pressure for an hour. It redirects your focus for a bit so that when you come back, you are refreshed. This is one of the main ways you will ensure that you will make it over the long haul.

Every day around 4:00 or 4:30 in the afternoon, I stop my work to go to the gym. Unless there is an emergency (a real emergency), I do not miss. When you prioritize your hobby this way, you are really prioritizing the health of your soul.

DON'T FEEL GUILTY

Most pastors feel guilty. I believe the source of this guilt is the expectations that have been placed on them by people in the community, in the church, or on staff. Many people who are in our churches have been in other churches before. This means that they come with some experience. Their last pastor had preached a certain way, used a certain version of the Bible, did the weddings at the church, oversaw who got to use the building and at what time, chose the songs for the Sunday worship service, answered all his emails the same day, and all his voicemails . . . and on and on. He also did all the premarital and marital counseling for the church as well as cut the grass.

You will never meet the expectations of your congregation. I repeat—never. When I came to this realization, it was like I was a new man. I discovered that leading a growing church has a lot to do with learning how to disappoint people at a rate they can handle. If you develop a new hobby or two, it will mean that you will no longer be able to do some of the things that you normally do for your people—and that is perfectly fine. In fact, if you want to grow your church without losing your soul, it is *required* that you stop doing most of the things you are currently doing. This doesn't mean that they don't get done. It means that they don't get done by you.

I'VE DISCOVERED THAT LEADING A GROWING CHURCH HAS A LOT TO DO WITH LEARNING HOW TO DISAPPOINT PEOPLE AT A RATE THEY CAN HANDLE.

On one random Sunday morning, a man in our church walked up to me in the lobby and said these words: "I realized something about you, Danny. You're a pretty good speaker, but you're not a very good pastor." Ouch! At the moment, those words hurt, but as I reflected on what he said, I came to realize that what he was really saying was that I wasn't very good at doing all of the things his previous pastor did—visiting hospitals, doing funerals, and performing weddings. And he was right!

To be clear, all of those things get done at our church, but I am rarely the one who is doing them. The offense didn't last very long, and our church kept on growing.

The key to not feeling guilty about your hobby is realizing that it is a major part of what is keeping you in the game. It is caring for your body and soul. The greatest gift you can give your church is a healthy you; therefore, you must prioritize your hobbies and not feel guilty for doing so. It is your responsibility.

To close this chapter, I would like to urge you not to kid your-self and think that a hobby is a luxury and that maybe when things slow down, you will think about starting a hobby. This is a dangerous way to think because it's this thinking that usually leads to a pastor waiting too long to learn healthy practices to deal with the stresses of ministry.

I would argue that a pastor should start with hobbies when the church is small. A pastor should create the habit of it before the church grows and becomes complicated. This will ensure that the system is prebuilt and habits are preset, allowing space for you to breathe, rest, and recover. Please do not wait. You are not the exception to the rule. You are just as human as the next person.

Chapter 9

DON'T DO IT ALONE— YOUR NEED FOR FRIENDS

In his book *Vital Friendships*, Tom Wrath shared about a time back in 1991 when he was invited to work on a special research project that aimed to help shelters and city missions develop better programs for people in need. The question he was tasked to answer was simple, "Why do some people emerge from homelessness and recover, while others do not?" He admits to thinking that this was not a hard question to answer since it was quite obvious that most people were homeless in large part due to excessive drug and alcohol abuse; however, as he dove deeper into the study, he discovered something he did not expect.

Alcoholism and drug addiction were indeed factors, but "in most cases, the relationship with the bottle or needle was predicated by the collapse of a close relationship with a friend or loved one." His study found that "men and women who remained homeless for decades had something in common: a lack of healthy friendships. They were more friendships than anything else."[40]

I have saved this chapter for last because I think it's true that people often remember the last thing that is said to them in a conversation. This topic is something I do not want you to forget. It just might save you and your ministry. I want to talk to you about the power of developing and maintaining healthy relationships.

THE BIBLE SAYS THAT DAVID WAS A GREAT WARRIOR, AND THAT HE KILLED TENS OF THOUSANDS. YES, HE DID. BUT HE DID NOT DO IT ALONE—AND NEITHER CAN YOU.

The truth is that if you are going to grow your church, develop your soul, and have staying power in ministry, you cannot do it without several good friends. In 2 Samuel 23, we read about David's "mightiest warriors." Verse 39 tells us, "There were thirty-seven in all." These were the men who went everywhere with David and fought alongside him against their enemies. Among the thirty-seven, there were three: Jashobeam the Hacmonite, Eleazar son of Dodai, and Shammah son of Agee. These three men were all Braveheart types, all of which achieved superhuman feats in battle. The Bible says that David was a great

40   Tom Rath, *Vital Friends: The People You Can't Afford to Live Without* (New York, NY: Gallup Press, 2006) 8.

warrior, and that he killed tens of thousands. Yes, he did. But he did not do it alone—and neither can you.

In their book *15 Characteristics of Effective Pastors*, Kevin Mannoia and Larry Walkemeyer point out that one of those characteristics is living in accountable relationships. They wrote:

> *Effective pastors have close friends with whom they share life. They are friends who are quick to challenge or to affirm the pastor toward godly character and personal excellence.*[41]

Being a pastor and having friends to do life with is hard. Having a healthy community of friends you can do life with is a primary struggle for pastors today. Finding this community can be quite a challenge. In their book *A Path to Belonging: Overcoming Clergy Loneliness*, Mary Kay DuChene and Mark Sundby point out that loneliness among clergy is an epidemic.[42] There are some key reasons for this.

A recent article in *Outreach* magazine about the top six struggles pastors face today expressed the struggle to find friends in a question: "How do you get into community with people who either put you too high on a pedestal or watch for your every fault and failure?"[43]

The overlap between ministry and friendship can pose a unique challenge for the pursuit of close relationships. If it is not navigated with wisdom and care, this overlap can be the source of all kinds of problems. Pastor Steven Witmer explains, "Our need to be available and always 'on' as our congregation's shepherd may

41 Kevin W. Mannoia and Larry Walkemeyer, *15 Characteristics of Effective Pastors: How to Strengthen Your Inner Core and Ministry Impact* (Grand Rapids, MI: Baker Books, 2011) 172.
42 Mary Kay DuChene and Mark Sundby, *A Path to Belonging: Overcoming Clergy Loneliness* (Minneapolis, MN: 1517 Media, 2022) .
43 Ed Stetzer, "Pastor, Don't Struggle Alone," *Outreach Magazine*, 27 Nov. 2019, outreachmagazine.com/features/leadership/49347-pastor-dont-struggle-alone.html.

squelch reciprocal friendships in which we ourselves are known, loved, and encouraged."[44]

When we develop friendships with the people we pastor, there can be and often are unrealistic expectations involved. They may have the expectation that all we do is talk about Jesus or the Bible in every conversation. They may expect that we don't have strong convictions about anything outside of the Bible; we don't drink alcohol, are always positive, always available to talk or help, never act selfishly or give in to anger, and on and on it goes. Pastors struggle to shake the feeling that they are working even when they are in social settings with friends. Developing friendships where expectations like these are dropped or diminished can seem like an impossible task. That may be the case, but no matter how hard it may seem, you must be willing to find a few people who will love you as you are and make space for you to be a normal person.

The alternative to friendship is loneliness. Loneliness in ministry can be and often is the reason pastors quit. Clergy coach Laura Stephens-Reed explains the danger of loneliness in a recent article: "People who feel lonely are at a 26 percent greater risk of premature death—a threat as great as if we smoked 15 cigarettes a day—and that is particularly true for those of us who are middle-aged."[45] Fifteen cigarettes a day! Holy smokes! That's dangerous. As it turns out, we need friendships as much as we need anything else to stay healthy. Being relationally connected to a few good friends is as important as a healthy diet and exercise routine!

---

44 Stephen Witmer, "Loneliness Limits Ministry: Why Pastors Need Good Friends," *Desiring God*, 15 July 2021, www.desiringgod.org/articles/loneliness-limits-ministry.

45 Laura Stephens-Reed on Daniel Potter's blog, "Pastors Are Lonely, and This Is a Big Problem," *CBFblog*, 18 May 2023, cbfblog.com/2023/05/18/pastors-are-lonely-and-this-is-a-big-problem/.

AS IT TURNS OUT, WE NEED FRIENDSHIPS AS MUCH AS WE NEED ANYTHING ELSE TO STAY HEALTHY.

Why do pastors struggle to develop friendships? Well, there isn't just one answer. Some of the reasons are the same reason other people struggle to have good friends. In a recent article, Pastor Steven Witmer wrote the following:

> *Why do many pastors find it so difficult? There are a lot of reasons, many of them not specific to pastors. Like other people, we're very busy, focused intently on work and family and home-improvement projects and our local community. We're independent and don't feel an urgent need to cultivate deep relationships. We're tired at the end of the day and want to cocoon at home. Some of us are natural introverts, preferring our own company to that of others. Some of us are insecure, not knowing quite how to go about the formation of friendships.*[46]

There are other reasons that are unique to pastors because of the dynamic of ministry. The challenges of ministry can be unlike any other challenges people face and, therefore, are hard for others to understand. How can a normal person understand and relate to the pressure of putting together a weekly thirty – to forty–minute presentation, talking with a couple who is about to get divorced, performing a funeral, working with staff members who

---

46 Stephen Witmer, "Loneliness Limits Ministry: Why Pastors Need Good Friends," *Desiring God*, 15 July 2021, www.desiringgod.org/articles/loneliness-limits-ministry.

cannot work out their differences, helping someone overcome an addiction to porn, and a high capacity financial supporter who is thinking about leaving because the lyrics of a worship song were not doctrinally sound? All in one week! It's hard for the average person to understand and relate to the life of a pastor.

SOMETIMES, IT'S THE EXPECTATIONS WE HAVE OF OTHERS THAT MAKE FRIENDSHIP HARD

Finding and keeping friends who can hold the same values and standards and commitments is very challenging. The act of holding a friend accountable to those expectations puts a strain on the relationship. Brandon Sutton, associate pastor of The Journey Church in Lebanon, Tennessee, shared his experience in a recent article on this subject:

> *At my previous church, there was a man whom I considered a good friend. We hung out at each other's homes. We went out to eat and to ball games together. We had a lot in common. But he was lazy in his faith. He didn't engage in the spiritual disciplines like Bible study and prayer. He rarely witnessed or discipled other men. His church attendance was inconsistent at best. He didn't lead his family well at all. What began to manifest is that our friendship often stood in the way of me having courage to tell him the truth as his pastor. When I did speak the truth to him (repeatedly), it hurt our friendship. The man eventually left my church, and we pretty much lost touch with one another. Given the superseding obligations I had to him as a shepherd, I found it difficult being both his pastor and his friend.*

It's hard for a pastor to have a friend. It's also hard to be the friend of a pastor. Let's face it—what we do is weird. It is multidimensional and multifaceted. If you tried to explain it to the average person, would they understand? Probably not. Because it's hard, we do the worst possible thing we could do. We stop trying. We back away. We withdraw, and we isolate. We become independent. We decide to keep everyone at arm's length and just be the pastor to all. We remain alone and unknown. There is only one problem. That's not how God made you.

I know, I know, I can hear you arguing with me. You have tried before to develop friends. You preached a sermon or a series on small groups and the value of doing life with other believers. You used Ecclesiastes 4:9-10 as your main text:

> *Two people are better off than one, for they can help each other succeed. If one person falls, the other can reach out and help. But someone who falls alone is in real trouble.*

The talk was a hit and landed really well, right? It was so convicting that you went first. You joined a group because you wanted to lead by example. And it worked—for a while. But then it didn't. You went deep, got vulnerable, got honest—and you got burned. The end result? You lost trust.

Maybe the friend turned on you and used your vulnerability and shortcomings against you. Maybe you were accused of favoritism. Maybe it was something you said in a sermon. Maybe the friend didn't like a decision you made within the church. I'm not sure, but somehow that friend hurt you, and you don't want to experience that pain again. So, to protect yourself, you resigned to never trying that again. It's understandable. It's a defense mechanism against pain. It's *also* a surefire way to take yourself right out of ministry.

How do I know this? Because I have lived through it. I have opened my heart to people in friendship, and I have been burned. And for a time, I withdrew and isolated myself. During these times of withdrawal, I noticed myself going backward—backward in my spiritual vitality, in my excitement about the church, and in my physical and emotional vitality.

GOD DID NOT DESIGN US FOR EMOTIONAL ISOLATION.

God did not design us for emotional isolation. In their book *Renegade Pastor*, Searcy and Jarman put it like this: "God created us to have close relationships. When we don't have those close relationships, we are actually living out of step with the way God created us."[47]

My heart grew more and more angry as I isolated myself from others. Not only was I aware that what I was doing was wrong, but I also became aware that my soul was slowly dying. If I hadn't made a change, I am convinced that I would not be in ministry today, and I most certainly would not be writing these words to you.

Today, I enjoy several different healthy relationships, and I feel connected to a strong group of men who are doing life with me.

---

47 Nelson Searcy, *The Renegade Pastor: Abandoning Average in Your Life and Ministry* (Grand Rapids, MI: Baker Books, 2015).

We have a group of elders at our church that I meet with once a month whom I genuinely love and trust. Beyond our elders, I also have two other groups of men I meet with. These guys are so important to me that they are worth mentioning by name: Rick, Don, Frank, Michael, Jesse, R.J., and Bill. These are men I meet with weekly or biweekly for fellowship, study, discussion, and accountability. We talk about everything and challenge each other to be the men God created us to be. They encourage my heart and strengthen my faith on a weekly basis. At this point in my life and ministry, I would never even try to lead my church and family without them. So, how do you get started in developing friendships?

THE FIRST STEP IS HUMILITY

Developing good friendships starts with humility. As a pastor, there is simply no way to manage the load of ministry by yourself. I have tried to remind myself that humility is having the appropriate view of oneself. And you, my friend, are not God. Unlike God, you have severe limitations. You must sleep, eat, and drink for starters. To think that you can manage to lead a ministry alone is delusional and a good sign that you might have a Messiah complex. You don't have the spiritual or emotional capacity to lead and grow a church without the support of good friends.

I'm not talking about the practical help a good staff provides. Yes, you need that. I am talking about the emotional support of friendship. In Genesis 2:18, God said, "It is not good for man to be alone." I know God is talking specifically about the reason He created Eve, but I don't think she is the only one to whom He was referring. Humble pastors know they cannot make it without others in their corners. However imperfect people are, Jesus works through them to provide help for the journey.

One of my favorite lines in the Old Testament is found in 1 Samuel 23:16, "Jonathan went to find David and encouraged him to stay strong in his faith in God." We know that David was a mighty man of faith, a man after God's own heart. His faith gave him the courage to take on a nine-foot giant! But even he faced moments in his life where he needed encouragement to keep the faith.

In one of the darkest times in his life, God provided a friend. Jonathan sought out David, found him, and encouraged David to keep his eyes on God. He helped him to continue to believe in the plan that God had for him. Like David, you and I need encouragement to stay strong in the dark times. We need encouragement to stay faithful to our calling to grow the church. Are you humble enough to admit your need? Humble enough to look for a Jonathan—or two?

THE NEED FOR STRENGTH

Several years ago, I read Dietrich Bonhoeffer's book, *Life Together*. One particular sentence surrounding the topic of friendship grabbed me and changed my thinking forever. He wrote, "The physical presence of other Christians is a source of incomparable joy and strength."[48] Wow! The right friend can provide "incomparable joy and strength." That means there is nothing else like it besides the very strength of God Himself. I became convinced. What you need is God's strength, but how does God deliver that strength?

---

48   Dietrich Bonhoeffer, *Life Together* (London, England: SCM Press, 1954) 19.

WHAT I HAVE COME TO REALIZE IS THAT ONE OF THE PRIMARY WAYS GOD DELIVERS STRENGTH TO PASTORS IS THROUGH PEOPLE.

Many times, strength comes through His Holy Spirit and through His Word. Sometimes strength comes through a song, sermon, or a book. What I have come to realize, however, is that one of the primary ways God delivers strength to pastors is through people. There is something almost unexplainable that can happen between friends in the midst of hard times. In his book, *The Power of the Other*, Henry Cloud tells a story about his brother-in-law Mark who had been a Navy SEAL that illustrates the power of a true friend:

> His teammate, whom I'll call Bryce, was in the ocean during Hell Week, swimming the last long leg to the finish line. Mark had already made it; he passed the final test and knew that he would become a SEAL. For him, it was done, and he was standing on the rocks above the water, eagerly watching his buddies strive toward the goal.
>
> That was when Bryce "hit the wall."
>
> As he described it, it was that moment when his body would just go no more. It was done. Nothing left. He tried to will himself to keep going, but his body would not obey. . . .
>
> As he told the story of going down, about to call for help and signal that it was over for him, his eyes fell upon the land ahead. There was Mark, standing on the shore. Mark saw him, and Bryce said that Mark gave him a huge fist

pump and a yell, signaling to Bryce that "he could do it." Their eyes locked for a few seconds, and as Bryce described it, something *happened.* Something beyond him. *His body jumped into another gear, into another dimension of performance that he had not had access to before; he was able to get back on top of the cold water again and swim toward the finish line. He made it. He finished. He would become a SEAL.*[49]

What a remarkable story and testimony to the power a friend can have in your life. The reality is that to isolate yourself from people is to cut yourself off from a major source of supernatural strength from heaven. The very strength you need to handle disappointing people, the loss of people to other churches, the constant trauma others are facing, your own insecurities and fears, and a host of other issues is denied when you isolate yourself. In order to find that strength, you need people. You need people who care about you deeply and can empathize in a real way. That means that you must open up and trust a few friends. There is no way around it. How much strength and staying power are you forfeiting by not prioritizing a few good friendships?

HOW MUCH STRENGTH AND STAYING POWER ARE YOU FORFEITING BY NOT PRIORITIZING A FEW GOOD FRIENDSHIPS?

---

49 Henry Cloud, *The Power of the Other* (New York, NY: Harper Collins, 2016), 5.

THE NEED FOR INSIGHT

Leading a growing church requires that you make good decisions and lots of them, which means that you must have keen insight on lots of issues. You need insight on the right people to hire, topics to cover in your sermons, how to talk about the challenges of ministry with your elders, how to address a shortfall of resources, or how to let a long-time staff member go. The decisions are endless. My insight on these issues is limited. My perspective is limited. So is yours. Neither you nor I can see clearly on all these things.

It is hard to see things the way we need to because we are emotional creatures. The emotions we experience, whether love, compassion, insecurity, or anger tend to fog our view. We are like most people when we are emotional, unable to see the right course of action. Isn't it interesting that when we are talking to other people about their problems, the answers seem to be very simple and clear? Why is that? We have none of the emotion attached to the situation.

A man came to me a few years ago in need of marriage counseling. He had gotten too close to one of his female coworkers and now had some deep feelings for her. His wife found out about the relationship, and, well, she was more than a bit concerned. My counsel to him was simple and sure to work. I advised him to leave his place of employment and stop speaking to this woman who was not his wife. What I witnessed was amazing. Even though his marriage was on the verge of being lost, he refused to leave his position and stop speaking to the other woman. I asked, "Why?" He told me the other woman was going through a tough period in her life, and that she would feel abandoned, and she needed him. He could not understand how the feelings of this woman were not his responsibility. I'm amazed at how misled we can be and how resistant we can be to wise counsel when we are emotional.

The power of heeding wise counsel cannot be understated. A few years ago, one of our staff members asked me to meet on a Friday. He knew it was my day off, so I knew it was serious. During the meeting, he proceeded to tell me that he had gotten too close to a woman in our congregation. After listening for a while, I told him exactly what he needed to do and gave him examples from Scripture to support what I was saying. I could tell he heard me, but something was off.

I probed a little bit, and he told me that he was thinking of leaving his wife for this other woman. It was rare for me to see someone—a good man, a godly man—so fooled. To make a long story short, he did not take my advice, was let go from our staff, and caused much pain in the lives of his family and friends.

But thankfully, that's not how the story ended. I stayed in contact with him, and others did as well. We never stopped praying for him and encouraging him. Months later, my friend came to his senses like the prodigal son, repented of his sin, and returned to his wife. God never gave up on him, and neither did we. Gently and sometimes bluntly, we reminded him of what he should do. This is what friends do and why you should surround yourself with them. Today, he is back together with his wife, their marriage is healing, and God is using him again in the church for His glory!

THE REALITY OF SPIRITUAL ATTACKS

As a pastor, you pose a threat to our "great enemy," as Peter refers to him in 1 Peter 5:8. You are the one who is leading the charge to help people enter the kingdom through faith in Jesus. If there is anyone the devil would love to destroy, it is you. In his book *Bondage Breaker*, Neil Anderson states, "If you're a Christian, you're a target. If you're in ministry, you're a bull's eye."[50]

We are in the midst of a great battle over souls, and our adversary is playing for keeps. You are his main prey. If he can take you out by tempting you to become ego-driven, lustful, greedy, discouraged, or angry, he will cause immeasurable pain and disillusionment in your church and the community you are trying to reach. His goal is to cause you and the church you lead to fail in reaching what God has intended in this broken world. No soldier in any army attempts to fight a war by himself. You will need some friends who will enter the battle with you.

Just because we are pastors doesn't mean that we aren't susceptible to the lies of the enemy whose goal is to steal, kill, and destroy (John 10:10). There is no better target than someone who has isolated themselves. We preach this stuff, but we don't always live it out. I'm not sure what the enemy has planned for me or what ideas he is going to try to plant into my mind and heart, but whatever is, I'm not facing it alone. Neither I nor you are a match for his deception.

WHERE TO START?

You start by making friendship a priority. For sure, your relationship with God, your spouse, and your kids come first. But friendship must be right behind these. All too often we use the pressures of ministry and our busy schedules as an excuse not to develop friendships. This is a mistake. The pressures of ministry

---

50 Neil T. Anderson and David Park, *The Bondage Breaker* (Eugene, OR: Harvest House Publishers, 2022).

and busyness of life will always be there. If you want to have friends, you must learn to place your relational needs before the needs of the church. Making friendship a priority means that you schedule it. Whatever does not get scheduled does not get done. I have one meeting with friends on Wednesday nights and another biweekly meeting on Friday mornings. You need consistent time together to build a friendship, and the only way to do that is to put it on the schedule. Obviously, this will not always work out. There will always be emergencies that will require our attention. We must let this be the exception and not the rule.

PICK A FEW GOOD FRIENDS

A few years ago, I decided to think through a short list of people that I would want to be friends with. The list included men who I knew for sure were men committed to their relationship with Christ, being a good husband and father, successful in their occupation, growth-minded, and possessing a high level of emotional intelligence. I wrote their names down and asked them if they were willing to get together on a regular basis to pursue spiritual growth together.

Each one of these men had a track record I could observe. All too often we leave friendship up to proximity and attention—who is around us because of our schedules and who likes us because of our role. We must be much more intentional than this. You are in a position to know who is really taking life seriously and who can add value to your life. So, make your list and seek them out to be your friends.

GIVE PERMISSION AND BE VULNERABLE

Once you've identified and sought out those few friends who will walk through life with you, if their friendship is truly going to add the value that it is intended to add, you must give them permission to speak. Giving permission to speak is going beyond being honest or transparent. There is a difference between being transparent and being vulnerable. When we are transparent, we are honest about what is going on. But when we are vulnerable, we have opened ourselves up to critique by giving the friends in our lives the freedom to speak.

If a friendship is going to add the value you need, you must have a conversation about what you expect and what is okay. I have found that unless you make it clear that the purpose of the friendship is to encourage, challenge, and strengthen one another, the friendship will remain shallow. You must look at the men in your life and tell them that they not only have permission to speak into your life but also that you are counting on them to do so. That is the point. After this is clear, you must go first and open up with something that is a struggle in your life that you need help with. You can start slowly with something like an organizational struggle or something that is troubling you with one of your children.

When you open up like this, it communicates that you are serious and that you are sincerely looking for insight and help. This requires that you take a risk and trust your friends. Trust is hard, especially if you have been burned; however, as you get better at choosing the right friends, you can reduce the risk. Again, the alternative of loneliness is not an option.

IF YOU KEEP YOUR HEART OPEN AND LOOK AROUND, GOD WILL SEND YOU A JONATHAN.

Inevitably, if you stay at your church for any significant length of time, you will have some key relationships that don't make it. The friend moves away and enters a new stage of life, or the friendship ends over some kind of disagreement. As a younger pastor, this would be a major source of pain. As I have grown and matured, God has shown me that I need to be grateful for the time I had with that person, for the value that the friend added over the years, and the value I added to them. It is rare to have a friend that will go the distance with you. That is okay. If you keep your heart open and look around, God will send you a Jonathan.

The challenges of friendship are difficult, but the alternative is not an option. It takes time, wisdom, and vulnerability. There will be some pain involved, for sure, but the rewards far outweigh the cost. Pay the cost. Get some friends. You're in a battle, and you can't do it alone.

A FINAL WORD

This book has been my attempt to help you grow your church without losing your soul. Far too many pastors have made numerical growth of their church the primary focus of their lives and neglected their inner condition. As a result, their character was not deep or wide enough to uphold or sustain the growth. These pastors had a good run but did not finish well and left behind much damage to their church, their community, their family, themselves, and the name of Jesus. On the other hand, many pastors have chosen to focus on their spiritual growth and the spiritual growth of the people they already pastor to the neglect of the thousands around them who do not know Christ. As a result, the community is not reached for Christ, and people just miles away languish without knowing Him.

My hope and prayer are that this book will equip you and serve as a guide to help you do both. It is possible to reach hundreds, even thousands, each and every week with the gospel while at the same time living and walking with Jesus in an intimate, growing relationship. Successful, fruitful ministry is an overflow of a heart that is well-ordered and centered on Jesus. I often tell pastors that the best gift you can give your church is not your sermons or your leadership but a healthy soul. Everything we do flows from our hearts.

IT IS POSSIBLE TO REACH HUNDREDS, EVEN THOUSANDS, EACH AND EVERY WEEK WITH THE GOSPEL WHILE AT THE SAME TIME LIVING AND WALKING WITH JESUS IN AN INTIMATE, GROWING RELATIONSHIP.

If this book can help you strike the balance of fruitful ministry and the maintenance of your soul, then it will have served its purpose. What I have put down in words is not merely random ideas that I have picked up from others; instead, they are words of wisdom that, if applied, really do work in real life. This book is filled with "practices" that I and my team have been implementing for over two decades. I am a practitioner, not a theorist. I want to know what works and what does not. If you will take a few of the ideas in this book and work them out in your own life, I believe you will see similar results.

What is at stake? Simply everything! Leading a growing church is a high-risk endeavor. Your reputation is on the line. Your relationship with your kids is on the line. Your emotional and mental well-being is on the line. Your marriage is on the line. The salvation of the lost people in your community is on the line.

I hope you can sense the gravity of my words. I cannot overstate it—the only real story going on today is the story of how

God is bringing people to Himself through faith in Jesus. If we get this wrong, the implications are severe; however, if we get it right—by caring for our souls, prioritizing our family, building our leadership skills, digging deep when times get hard, always improving, taking care of our bodies, developing life-giving hobbies, and choosing not to do life without some good friends—well, then the kingdom will be advanced, and the world will reflect a little more of what God originally intended when He created it.

In the first chapter of this book, I said that the world is a hungry place. The world is a desperate place. The world is a starving place. We have what the world needs and that is the life-changing gospel of Jesus. He is the Living Water. He is the Bread of Life. He is what the world needs now more than ever.

God's plan for you is twofold. First, He desires you to be His disciple and find in Him everything you need and experience everything for which you were created. You are to live and work with Him every day, enjoying His presence as you bear His "easy" yoke. He wants you to be filled with peace, love, and joy as you lead, pastor, and preach to His people. Your life is to be the example of the kind of life in the kingdom into which you are inviting people. If this is to be a reality, you must be seeking Him every day and caring for your soul. In a real sense, you are the "product." The gospel of Jesus must be working in you first, changing you and transforming you, *before* it can work for anyone else.

Secondly, it is God's will that more and more people enter His kingdom through faith in His Son. He has called His church to reach the world, and the world is a very big place. You and your church are part of that plan, as is mine. The church is His method of reaching the world. He has called you to use your voice, your leadership, and your influence to build His family—one that will live with Him and worship Him forever.

THE GOSPEL OF JESUS MUST BE WORKING IN YOU FIRST, CHANGING YOU AND TRANSFORMING YOU, *BEFORE* IT CAN WORK FOR ANYONE ELSE.

What a privilege and what an honor we share! You must learn all that you need to learn in order for more and more people to enter into His kingdom. This will require all of your effort and God's help. It can be done. It will be done. The only question I ask you is, "How big of a role will you play in God's story?" Yes, that depends on how well you hone your leadership skills, but more importantly, it depends on how well you care for your heart. Pastor, you can, in fact, grow your church without losing your soul.

www.ingramcontent.com/pod-product-compliance
Lightning Source LLC
Chambersburg PA
CBHW070539090426
42735CB00013B/3028